C0-CEG-499

The World of Motorcycles

AN ILLUSTRATED ENCYCLOPEDIA

COLUMBIA HOUSE/New York

Editor:	Ian Ward
Editorial Director:	Brian Laban
Assistant Editors:	Laurie Caddell
	Brian Laban
	Mike Winfield
Editorial Assistants:	Jenny Dawson
	Michael Maxwell
Art Editor:	Andrew Weall
Picture Editor:	Mirco Decet
Picture Researcher:	Clive Gorman
Cover Photo:	C. May; S. & G.
	Press Agency
Design:	Harry W. Fass
Production:	Stephen Charkow

Picture acknowledgments
Page 2522—2531: Motor Cycle—2532: Quattroruote—2533: Quattroruote—2534: Motor Cycle—2535: Motor Cycle—2536: Motor Cycle; N. Nicholls—2537—2541: N. Nicholls—2542: Motor Cycle—2543: Motor Cycle—2544: Quattroruote; J. Heese—2545: J. Heese—2546: N. Nicholls—2547: L.J. Caddell; N. Nicholls; N. Nicholls; Motor Cycle—2548: Cecil Bailey—2549: Cecil Bailey—2550: Publifoto—2551: Quattroruote; Publifoto—2552: Publifoto—2553: S. Lancefield—2554: F. Zagari; F. Zagari; Quattroruote—2555: Quattroruote—2556: Motor Cycle; N. Nicholls—2557: Motor Cycle; N. Nicholls; N. Nicholls—2558: Motor Cycle—2559: National Motor Museum—2560: Motor Cycle—2561: N. Nicholls; Motor Cycle—2562: Publifoto—2563: Quattroruote—2564: R. Shelby—2565: R. Shelby; Motor Cycle—2566: National Motor Museum; Motor Cycle—2567: Motor Cycle—2568: N. Nicholls—2569: N. Nicholls —2570: Motor Cycle—2571: N. Nicholls—2572: Quattroruote; Keig Collection; Quattroruote—2573: Quattroruote—2574: Publifoto; Keystone Press; Le Moto—2575: Quattroruote—2576: N. Nicholls—2577: N. Nicholls—2578: Motor Cycle—2579: Motor Cycle; Keig Collection—2580: N. Nicholls—2581: N. Nicholls—2582: N. Nicholls—2583: N. Nicholls; F. Zagari— 2584: N. Nicholls; J. Heese—2585: N. Nicholls—2586: N. Nicholls; Motor Cycle; Motor Cycle—2587: N. Nicholls— 2588: N. Nicholls—2589: N. Nicholls— 2590: N. Nicholls—2591: N. Nicholls; Quattroruote; Quattroruote—2592: C. May— 2593: S & G Press Agency—2594: Motor Cycle; N. Nicholls—2595: N. Nicholls; N. Nicholls; Motor Cycle; Motor Cycle; N. Nicholls—2596: N. Nicholls—2597: Motor Cycle; N. Nicholls—2598: Motor Cycle— 2599: Motor Cycle; Keig Collection—2600: C. May; Syndication International—2601: C. May—2602: Motor Cycle—2603: N. Nicholls; Motor Cycle; N. Nicholls; Motor Cycle—2604: N. Nicholls; J. Lloyd; N. Nicholls—2605: N. Nicholls; N. Nicholls; J. Lloyd—2606: Motor Cycle; N. Nicholls— 2607: Motor Cycle; N. Nicholls—2608: Publifoto—2609: Publifoto—2610: N. Nicholls; Keig Collection—2611: N. Nicholls; Motorcycle News—2612: N. Nicholls; J. Greening; Motor Cycle—2613: J. Lloyd; Motor Cycle; N. Nicholls—2614: N. Nicholls—2615: Publifoto; N. Nicholls— 2616: Keystone—2617: N. Nicholls—2618: Motor Cycle—2619: Quattroruote—2620: A. Edwards/Motorcycle News—2621: C. May —2622: Motor Cycle.

© IGDA—Novara—1976 and 1977   ISBN 0 85613 3612
© Orbis Publishing Ltd., London, 1979
Distributed by Columbia House, a Division of CBS Inc., 1211 Avenue of the Americas, New York, New York 10036
Printed in U.S.A.

Contents   Page

The history of motor cycle sport is rich in characters and legends. Sadly, for many of today's young enthusiasts, the achievements of these great men have been lost in the swirling mists of time. Without these men, however, the story of motor cycle competition would be incomplete, so here we begin a 'who's who' of all these heroes.

Ray Amm

Right: Rhodesian Ray Amm was one of the first colonials to make his name in motor cycle racing

Far right top: Amm aboard the 'kneeler' Norton at the 1953 North West 200, where he set the fastest lap

Far right bottom: He joined the Norton team in 1952, and raced in a number of European events, and is seen here competing in the 500cc Belgian Grand Prix

Below: Amm on the 'kneeler' Norton in 1953 at Montlhéry, where he set the fastest lap time and took the one-hour record at 133.71 mph

Ray Amm arrived in Europe from Southern Rhodesia in 1951 with a brace of Nortons and a driving ambition to earn himself a place in the world famous Norton works team. With a huge van, generally driven by his wife Jill, he joined the Continental circus and raced all over Europe.

He was soon spotted by Norton's brilliant team builder, Joe Craig, and in 1952 realised his initial objective by joining the Norton squad. When Geoff Duke left Norton for Gilera in 1953, Amm took over as team leader.

He was a fiercely determined rider. What he lacked in style he made up for in total dedication and sheer bravery. His assault on the Isle of Man in that first year as team leader was memorable, and brought him the Junior and Senior TT double, only the fifth rider to that time to achieve the distinction in one year. With almost total disregard for personal safety, he thundered after Geoff Duke's Gilera in the Senior event. He caught and passed him on the Mountain climb and descent, breaking course and lap records on his way to victory. His third and fastest lap at 97.41mph was almost 3mph faster than Duke's previous record.

In the Junior that year he led all the way to finish in record time. Good performances in Holland and Belgium helped him to third place in the 350cc world championship.

On the Island the following year he almost repeated his TT double of '53. In the Junior event, riding the 'Proboscis' Norton (so named for its peculiarly shaped forward-projecting frontal fairing), he led until the last lap, when the engine failed and he was robbed of certain victory. Earlier he had pushed his own 350cc lap-record up to 94.61mph.

In the Senior, which turned out to be one of

the wettest post-war TTs, Amm led the field, including Duke on the Gilera, when the race was dramatically abandoned after 151 miles. Again he set the fastest lap, at 89.82mph.

Ray Amm was doggedly patriotic and repeatedly turned down tempting contracts from the Italian factories, preferring to ride only British machines. For a couple of seasons he was the only Norton rider able to challenge the superiority of his former team mate Geoff Duke on the fast, multi-cylinder Gilera, and against almost overwhelming odds managed to secure runner-up positions in both the 350cc and 500cc world championships of 1954.

But as the tide turned completely against the single-cylinder Nortons, his passion to win took priority. Reluctantly he signed for the Italian MV-Agusta factory, but tragically his career was almost at an end. In his first race for MV, in the 350cc event at Imola on Easter Monday, 1955, he crashed on a slippery second-gear corner and was killed.

In his brief, but memorable career, (he was 29 when he died) he had taken the 'kneeler' Norton to Montlhéry in 1953 and captured the One Hour record at 133.71mph – over 6mph faster than Piero Taruffi's record of 1939 set on a supercharged Gilera! Earlier he established for Norton a new 350cc lap record at the North-West 200 event in Northern Ireland, before having to retire on lap three.

Slim and religious, Ray Amm had a fearless and abandoned style which produced many palpitating moments. He was obsessed by racing and the late Bob McIntyre once said: 'I never heard him talk of anything else.' A true gentleman, he was deeply respected for his skills, devotion and outstanding courage. Doubtless his tragic death was a great loss to motor cycle racing.   PC

Fergus Anderson

Below: Anderson in action on a Moto Guzzi; he was a works Moto Guzzi rider from 1950 until 1955, during which time he won two world titles for the Italian factory

Fergus Anderson was born in Britain, although it's hardly surprising that he was perhaps better known in Europe. He spent his most successful racing years there, in the 1950s, living in Italy and competing in Grand Prix events as a works rider for Moto Guzzi.

He began racing before the war and over the years rode a variety of machines including Rudge, Velocette, NSU and DKW. He was one of the first British riders to realise that he could probably make more money by racing regularly in Grand Prix events on the Continent, and formed with Ted Mellors and others what was probably the first 'Continental circus'.

In 1950 he signed for Moto Guzzi and was second in the 250cc world championship two years later. In 1953 he was third in the same class. It was largely Anderson who alerted the Italian factory to the potential for them in 350cc racing and urged them to produce a 350 version of their highly successful four-valve 250. At first there was little response and Anderson was left to contest the 350cc class with a machine which was literally an oversized 250. This 320cc Guzzi, however, was replaced by a true 350 which Anderson raced to the world title in 1953 in its first year of existence.

He was World Champion again in 1954 and although scarcely seen in Britain, competed on the Isle of Man, giving Guzzi victory in the lightweight 250cc TT in 1952 and '53. He had first competed there

in 1939 riding DKWs in the Senior and Junior races.

He was on the Continent in the 'thirties and almost until the outbreak of World War II was working as a journalist in Hamburg. Later he was to become well known for his 'Continental Chatter' column in the British weekly *Motor Cycle*.

After wartime naval service, he returned to racing on the Continent and in 1947 won the 350cc Swiss Grand Prix, that year also designated the Grand Prix d'Europe, on a Velocette he had purchased from the factory. His first World Championship, only four years after the FIM had reorganised the European title as a 'world' series, was the first in the 350cc class by a non-British machine, Velocette and Norton previously sharing the honours.

He soon became Moto Guzzi's number one rider and for six years lived with his wife and family on the edge of Lake Como in Italy, close to the Moto Guzzi factory.

He retired from racing to head Guzzi's competition department, but in 1955 quit the job on a point of principle after asking for a freer hand in the running of the team.

By now he was 47, but he wanted to ride again. He approached NSU in Germany, without success, but was offered a works 500 by BMW. In 1956 he was riding the BMW in an international meeting at Floreffe in Belgium. While chasing John Surtees he hit a patch of gravel, was thrown off and killed. **PC**

Above: Fergus Anderson, riding a Moto Guzzi, won the 250cc event at Bremgarten in Switzerland in 1952

Left: Fergus Anderson on his way to victory in the 1954 Dutch 350cc Grand Prix; he also won the Swiss, Italian and Spanish events that year

Hugh Anderson

Above: Anderson's AJS takes off over Ballaugh Bridge during the Isle of Man Junior TT of 1960. This was his first season in Europe.

Inset: Hugh Anderson, four times World Champion who specialised in racing small capacity machines

Hugh Anderson, born in New Zealand in 1936, won four World Championships during his career and is best remembered for his achievements on small capacity racers.

Anderson began his European racing career in the early 1960s riding the British four-stroke AJS and Norton machines. In 1961 he rode a Manx Norton into sixth place in the Italian Grand Prix and also scored a seventh place in that year's Isle of Man TT 350cc event.

The following year, 1962, saw Anderson being approached by the Japanese Suzuki factory, then planning a major assault on World Championship Grand Prix events. Anderson quickly learned to adapt his riding style to the technique needed for the smaller two-stroke machines and, on the tiny 125cc Suzuki, took sixth place in France and followed this up with a fifth place in Ulster and a fine first in the Argentine Grand Prix.

It was in 1963 that Anderson hit the jackpot as far as his career was concerned. Suzuki had developed their 50cc racer into a real winner while their 125cc machine was a new disc-valve model which was to prove a world beater. On these two new machines Anderson swept the board, finishing the season as both 50cc and 125cc World Champion. In the 50cc class Anderson won the Argentine Grand Prix and finished second in the Spanish, Dutch, Japanese and Isle of Man TT events while in the 125cc events Anderson was even more successful, winning the French, Dutch, German, Ulster and Finnish Grands Prix as well as the Isle of Man TT.

By 1964, the Japanese factories were taking

the small capacity classes very seriously and things were much harder for Anderson. Honda had introduced a new four-cylinder 125cc machine which Suzuki could not match. Consequently Luigi Taveri won the 125 title for Honda while Anderson could only manage third spot in the table.

In the 50cc class, however, Anderson and Suzuki were invincible and he swept to his third world title with wins at Daytona, France, Finland and the Isle of Man. He also finished second at Barcelona and third at Spa in Belgium to complete a very successful season.

In 1965, Suzuki re-designed their 125cc twin and it proved to be quicker than its rivals, so much so that Anderson won no less than six Grands Prix (the American, German, Spanish, French, Finnish and Japanese) to scoop his fourth World Championship title. Ironically, Anderson and Suzuki had little success in the 50cc category and he scored only one win – at the Spanish Grand Prix.

The following year, 1966, was a difficult and depressing year for Anderson. In the 125cc class, Honda had introduced their incredible five-cylinder machine and Anderson and his Suzuki were no match for Switzerland's Luigi Taveri. And in the 50cc class Anderson encountered another problem – his own team mate Hans-Georg Anscheidt who beat both the Honda team and Anderson to win his first world title.

At the end of 1966 Anderson declared that road racing was getting too dangerous and he retired. He took up motocross for fun for a couple of seasons and, following that, returned to Assen in Holland where he ran a motor cycle business. MW

Above left: Hugh Anderson in action at the 125cc Isle of Man TT of 1963 on his Suzuki. This was one of six Grand Prix wins scored by Anderson that year on his way to becoming World Champion

Below left: Anderson's Suzuki leads a gaggle of 50cc machines on his way to second place in the 1963 Dutch Grand Prix

Reg Armstrong

If only for one particular TT episode, Dublin-born Reg Armstrong deserves a special page in the golden book of road racing. The occasion was the 1952 Senior TT, the bike a works Norton; and as the chequered flag swept down to welcome home Reg as winner of the seven-lap event he eased back the throttle – and the primary chain snapped and fell into the roadway, right on the finish line.

Well, perhaps Armstrong was lucky enough to be born at just the right period, and to reach racing maturity at a point in time when the big motor cycle factories were vying for the services of top-class riders. His career spanned no more than eleven years (he retired at the comparatively early age of 28, to devote his time to building-up a thriving motor cycle business in Dublin) but for eight of those years he was a professional racer, variously under the banners of AJS, Norton, Gilera of Italy, and NSU of Germany.

Reg was, and indeed is, a man of particularly smart and tidy appearance, and this tidiness extended also to his riding style. None of your present-day knee-out, off-the-bike cornering. He stayed flat down and tucked in.

Starting as a 17-year-old in the multiplicity of minor Irish meetings that characterised the late 1940s, Armstrong made his way not by the adoption of hell-for-leather tactics, but by setting himself a schedule of advancement. He would select a couple of riders just a shade better than himself and make it his aim to improve his riding until he could beat them. Then two more riders were chosen, a bit better still; and so, painstakingly, rung by rung up the ladder to fame, if not fortune.

Right: Armstrong is congratulated by Geoff Duke and a crowd of well wishers after winning the 1952 Isle of Man Senior TT

That was quite typical of his mental approach to racing, and it certainly overcame the feeling of despair with which the average novice surveys the stars far above him. Even when he, too, was a star, Reg went no faster than was absolutely necessary to secure a victory. It was never in his temperament to go flat-out from the start.

The AJS factory was the first to recognise his talents by signing him to ride works machinery, and for a couple of years he campaigned the 500cc Porcupine twin with modest success (second place in the 1951 Swiss Grand Prix was possibly his best showing). But it was as a back-up man to superstar Geoff Duke, at first on Nortons and later on Gilera fours, that Reg Armstrong really came into his own and showed the racing world his true form.

It suited Reg to stay back while Duke went out as front runner, ready to take over should matters not go according to plan. In that 1952 Senior TT, for example, Geoff Duke led for four laps, until his clutch gave up. Armstrong had lain third, about half a minute behind Les Graham's howling MV Agusta four, but when Duke dropped out he turned on the pressure, to pass and lead Graham by just 4 seconds as the final lap began, and forge still further ahead to cross the line – minus that chain – just under half a minute to the good, proving his unquestionable ability to win in the face of adversity.

But the luck of the Irish ran out a month or two later, when Armstrong was leading the Ulster Grand Prix. Again the primary chain broke, but this time the finish was 2½ miles away. It cost Reg the chance of the highly prestigious 1952 500cc World Championship title.   FG

Left: Reg Armstrong (Velocette, number 52) leads Geoff Duke (Norton) during the 1950 350cc Grand Prix of Switzerland

Below: Armstrong in action on a Gilera four during the 1953 500cc Italian Grand Prix at the famous circuit of Monza

Artie Bell

Far right: Artie Bell takes off over Ballaugh Bridge during his victorious ride in the 1950 Junior TT race on his factory Norton

Below: Artie Bell pictured after the Isle of Man TT in 1949. Two years earlier, Bell had been invited to join the works Norton team

PACKED TIGHTER than rush-hour tube travellers, the 1950 Belgian Grand Prix 500cc field leant in unison into a second-lap corner – but then came tragedy. Leading the group on his works Gilera four, Carlo Bandirola changed line unexpectedly. Right behind him, Les Graham on the AJS Porcupine twin just touched the Gilera's rear wheel and went sprawling, dropping his machine right in the path of the works Norton pair, Geoff Duke and Artie Bell. It looked as though an accident was unavoidable.

There was nowhere for Artie Bell to go, and he and the Norton finished up tangled with the supporting pillars underneath a radio commentator's box.

In time Bell did survive his horrific crash; but it left him with a permanently useless left arm, and his all-too-brief career as a works road racer was at an abrupt and sad end.

Brief career, indeed, because Artie was already gone 32 years old when fellow-Ulsterman Joe Craig, supremo of Norton's Bracebridge Street racing department, invited him to join the official squad for 1947. But in the next three seasons Artie hit the heights. Riding in both 350 and 500cc classes, he scored two Isle of Man TT victories, two seconds, two thirds and a fourth.

Yet he had never even seen the tricky Isle of Man course before 1947, the year in which he confounded the pundits by leading the Senior TT on three of the seven laps. It was a remarkable performance, even for the talented Bell.

Artie's motor cycling had begun in his teenage years, and against strong opposition from his haulage-contractor father, who forced the youngster to dispose of the Model 9 Sunbeam he had bought. Of course, that didn't stop Bell, who continued to ride in minor events on an AJW-Python which, ostensibly, was owned by a friend. Unfortunately that subterfuge was shown up when the police stopped young Artie for riding with an ineffective silencer. Again there was a parental row, but in time Artie's persistence won through, and dad accepted his son's infatuation with bikes as something that just had to be endured.

It is worth noting that Artie had won £2 and a cup at a local fairground, by looping the Cage of Death on a positively prehistoric Vindec. But road racing was his real ambition, and by 1938 he had progressed sufficiently to finish in second place behind the great Bob Foster in the North-West 200 held in Northern Ireland.

With the resumption of Irish road racing in 1945, Artie Bell began to clean up with his 1939 Norton, his wins including Carrowdore, Cookstown, and the 500cc class of the Ulster Grand Prix. In addition, he had teamed up with the McCandless brothers in an agricultural and industrial machinery importing business, and it was the McCandless connection with Nortons (they designed and developed the Featherbed frame) which led eventually to a place in the works team. In those days, of course, riding for Norton was a major honour.

Yet it wasn't all road racing, because Artie was a real all-rounder who could count among his achievements the winning of the Patland Cup Trial, and qualification for the British Experts Trial; a ride in the Scott Trial; riding at Brands Hatch when that was a big-time grass-track venue; competing in show events as a horseman; and winning the Circuit of Ireland car rally. Competition careers don't come more varied than that. FG

Alec Bennett

Far right: Bennett poses with his Norton. In 1924, Bennett scored a classic hat trick of wins for Norton at the Isle of Man Senior TT, and the French and Belgian Grands Prix

Below: Alec Bennett on his way to a convincing win in the 1922 Isle of Man Senior TT on his twin-cylinder Douglas. During the race, Bennett set a new lap record of 59.99mph

POSSIBLY THE most unusual facet of Alec Bennett's racing career concerned the scarcity of his actual race appearances. In the nine-year spell (1921 to 1929) in which he was active in first-class competition, he rode in only 29 events. Yet his impact was undeniable, with thirteen major wins to his credit, eleven of those in international classics.

Born in Craigantlet, Belfast, in 1898, he emigrated as a boy to British Columbia, but returned to Britain soon after the outbreak of World War I.

Alec's early motor cycle experience had been on the half-mile dirt tracks of Western Canada, and at the age of sixteen he was already holder of the British Columbia Championship. He never did go back to Canada, and on demobilisation he elected to stay in England, obtaining a job as a motor cycle road-tester with the Sunbeam factory at Wolverhampton.

Really, that was a means to an end, and soon he had been drafted into the Sunbeam race team, alongside Tommy de la Hay, and the great George Dance. His first-ever road race was the 1921 Senior TT, in which he thrilled spectators (and caused the team manager to tear out his hair in handfuls) by using his dirt-track background to broadside the corners feet-up.

After four laps Alec led the field, but then a missed gear change led to a stretched valve and the Sunbeam's engine lost power. Bennett stopped, and tried to make roadside adjustments, but to no avail, and he had to console himself with a slower average speed and eventual fourth place.

All the same, he was lucky to have been able to race at all. During one of the practice sessions, carried out in a howling gale, a gust of wind caught Bennett and the Sunbeam as he approached the Gooseneck and he slammed into a stone wall, receiving severe concussion. After a few days in bed, and against doctor's orders, he came to the starting line with a safety helmet covering his heavily bandaged head.

If 1921 had brought disappointment, there was compensation the following year when, again on a Sunbeam, he won the Senior TT by more than 3½mph, at the same time setting a new lap record of 59.99mph. At that time, the '60 barrier' was regarded in much the same light as the 'ton barrier' in the 1950s, and not for another couple of years was the 60mph lap to be broken officially, by Jimmie Simpson. Later in 1922 Bennett moved west to the Douglas works at Bristol, where the new dropped-frame race model was under development. His Douglas period was an unhappy one, however, with the only win of note coming in the 100-mile Welsh Championships held on Pendine Sands. The 1923 Senior TT was run off in drenching rain, and even though he had lost his front mudguard Alec plodded on doggedly, eventually crossing the finishing line soaked to the skin to find the place absolutely deserted; not a soul in the grandstand, no welcoming marshal with the chequered flag, not even a bar attendant in the refreshment marquee. Fed up with the conditions, everybody had gone home bar him.

For some little while Alec Bennett had been planning to leave the motor cycle industry and, instead, go into business for himself as a dealer. Accordingly, in 1924 he opened the Southampton business which still bears his name, and it was largely because he had to concentrate his energies on making a go of it, that he rationed his racing.

Nevertheless, it was as a free-lance racer under the Norton banner that, in 1924, he had one of his best-ever seasons, pulling off the 'classic' hat-tricks of the Senior TT, and the French and Belgian Grands Prix. It was, incidentally, Norton's first TT win since 1907; but it was only Alec's determination that brought it off. Early in the race his fuel tank filler neck had broken off, and he had to stuff the gaping hole with a handkerchief, and stop to refuel every lap.

In the years ahead Bennett was to be seen less and less, but he did give Velocette their first-ever win with the overhead-camshaft engine in the 1926 Junior TT, repeating the performance two years later. For 1929 he was back on his old love, the Sunbeam, taking second place in the Senior TT.

He was to make one more appearance, in the 1932 Junior, finishing eighth. But Alec realised that he was getting no younger and, perhaps rather regretfully, he hung up his helmet. FG

Dave Bickers

ON 17 JANUARY 1978, Dave Bickers will have reached something of a milestone, though he will probably shy away from telling anyone about it. First, it will be his fortieth birthday, and second, it will be the start of his twenty-fifth year of competitive motor cycle racing.

To most people in Britain, the name Bickers will be familiar from television screens, where he still reigns as the man who has won more BBC trophy races than any other scrambler. Such film glory, however, is but a tiny part of the whole picture. As far as off-road motor cycle racing goes, Bickers has ridden in virtually every type of event in his career, and won in most of them. Some least-known successes include ice-racing, trials riding, in both solo and sidecar classes, and sidecar scrambling as well as solo scrambling for which he is better remembered.

The Bickers story began in 1953 when, at the age of fifteen, he got his hands on a 197cc Dot scrambler to practice in the fields near his home at Coddenham, near Ipswich. For many years he had been a spectator at nearby Shrubland's Park, scene of some of the great battles of British scrambling in the early 1950s. Having got the bug, young David decided it was time to try his hand himself. The following year, when he was old enough to get a racing licence, he entered his first event, and won his first heat.

Over the next two years, as he built up his experience, both in trials and scrambling, he rode a BSA, and then a Jawa. It was in 1956 that his rising talents came to the attention of the then thriving British factories, and it was Dot who gave him his first works ride. The young Bickers soon began to make an impression on the national circuit.

It was during that time that the stylish teenager caught the attention of Brian Stonebridge, possibly the greatest rider of his day, and later tragically killed in a car accident. Under Stonebridge's influence the

Far right: Dave Bickers (400 CZ) ploughs through the mud at the BBC Trophy meeting at Waterlooville, 1966

Below: Bickers on his CZ at the West Essex Linford scramble in 1968

young Bickers was offered a works ride by Greeves in 1958, and a partnership began that was to become world famous.

Greeves sent Bickers out to race abroad, and in his first year, 1959, he finished eighth in the European Championship. Having got the taste of continental competition, there was no stopping him. At the start of the 1960 season, he took the 250cc Greeves to the first Grand Prix of the year in Switzerland, won it, and went on to be the first, in fact still the only Briton, to take the title. He took it again in 1961, beating Arthur Lampkin for the crown.

Having won everything, he became bored with the championship and gave the 1962 series a miss, returning in 1963, when it had been upgraded to a World title chase, only to find the competition a lot stiffer, and his old Greeves no longer competitive.

He rode a semi-works Husqvarna for a while, later to return to Greeves when they came up with a new model, and added yet another British Championship to his total.

The next big turn in his career came in 1966 when he was signed up by CZ to contest the 500cc World Championship on their new 39bhp 360cc machine. He also became British importer for the Czech machines. In that year he came close to being the first man to take both 500 and 250cc British titles in the same season. He took the 500, but lost the 250 by just one point.

The international racing with CZ took him all over the world, and into a lot of extraordinary situations – including being arrested in Russia. Apart from the Grands Prix themselves, he raced in South Africa, Australia, New Zealand, and, along with team-mate Joel Robert, became one of the ambassadors of the sport who introduced motocross to the United States through the summer Inter Am and autumn Trans Am series. In 1968, with a sixth place at the Austrian Grand Prix at Launsdorf, he announced his official retirement from World Championship racing – the end of nine years in which he had not failed to finish in the first six of either the 250 or the 500cc class.

He continued to race internationally, just for fun, both regularly on the continent and in America, losing none of the flair and natural style which has been a hallmark of his career. In 1977, at the ripe old age of 39, Bickers was still graded among the top thirty solo scramblers for the British Championship.

By 1977 he was no longer CZ importer, that having been taken over by the Czechs themselves. He ran his own motor cycle and accessory business, and still rode in motocross and in enduros.　MC

George Brown

IN THE SPORT of sprinting no name is more venerated than that of George Brown. Throughout the fifties and sixties, George had consistently been the fastest straight line motor cyclist in England. His machines, the 998cc Nero and the 1147cc Super Nero, had taken him to numerous world and national records in the 1000cc and 1300cc categories.

George's allegiance to Vincent machines started in 1934 when, at 22 years of age, he started work at the Vincent factory in Stevenage. When the first 1000cc machine was produced in 1937, George was a factory tester. Much of his working week was spent riding the super fast bikes on public roads, and at weekends he rode the works racers in hill climbs, sprints and road races. His own 1000cc racer, which he christened 'Gunga Din', was used for all forms of the sport, and was the prototype of the famous Black Lightning racer which was reportedly capable of 180mph. On one occasion when he was appearing on a speeding charge, the magistrate threw the case out of court when he refused to believe that a motor cycle could travel so fast.

In 1951 Brown left the Vincent factory, which itself closed down shortly after. George was already the top man at most sprints and hill climbs, and in 1953 he quit road racing to concentrate on beating the clock. He built himself a 1000cc sprint machine out of a crashed bike. Not surprisingly it was another Vincent, although George had modified the engine and fitted Velocette rear and AJS front forks. He replaced the crankshaft with one of his own design

Right: the father figure of sprinting, George Brown was eventually forced out of competition by the FIM'S age rule

Below: in 1967 on his 1300cc, supercharged, vee-twin Vincent sidecar outfit

and upped the compression ratio to 15:1. As the bike had been built from the ashes of a burnt-out wreck he named it Nero (although 'Phoenix' may have been a more appropriate designation); fuelled it with alcohol or nitro-methane, and set out after records.

By 1961 Nero had been through many rebuilds and modifications. With an Avon slick rear tyre, a chopped and stretched frame and a dustbin fairing, he took his first world records. He clocked 108.74mph over the kilometre and, with an outrigger wheel fitted, he took the sidecar record to 98.98mph. Three years later he clocked an impressive 172.64mph over the flying kilo.

Not content with only one class to compete in, George built himself Super Nero, an 1147cc machine similar to Nero with which he began to take 1300cc class records. He also ran a very fast Ariel Arrow in the 250cc class with some success. His supercharged Vincent, however, which he built in 1967, never performed as well as the two Neros, which had held almost all the big capacity records throughout the sixties; one of the fastest of which was 189.33mph for the flying kilo.

In 1967 George was 55-years-old, the compulsory retirement age under FIM rules. At his last world meeting at Greenham Common, George retired in style with seven world and nine national records. Four years later he broke his last national record, and retired from the sport to run a motor cycle shop in Stevenage. GE

Above: George Brown was for many years the undisputed king of British sprint racing on his supercharged Vincents

Left: George Brown in action on Nero, his world famous sprint machine

Ralph Bryans

BORN IN NORTHERN IRELAND in 1948, Ralph Bryans was a racing star and World Champion in the 1960s. This was when motor cycle road racing gained a new dimension following the involvement of Japanese factories with their huge investment programmes in racing and lucrative rider contracts.

In his early career, Bryans took part in almost all branches of motor cycle sport, but decided to switch seriously to road racing in 1962. Earlier he had won his class on a 197cc Ambassador Villiers in the Irish Tandragee-100 event and, on a Norton, finished second on handicap in the Skerries 100. In 1962, he was ninth in the 350cc Ulster GP.

Bryans' first big break came in 1963 when he signed for Bultaco after a couple of convincing test rides in Spain: but an even bigger opportunity dropped into his lap almost immediately after through the intervention of Jim Redman. The Honda team leader had been impressed with Ralph Bryans' potential and got the famous Japanese factory to offer a much bigger contract than anything Bultaco could match. Bultaco appreciated the Irish rider's dilemma and sportingly agreed to release him from their contract.

In 1964, his first year as a works rider, Bryans won four Grands Prix – in Holland, Belgium, West Germany and Japan – and finished a remarkable second to Hugh Anderson in the 50cc world championship. His performance was all the more outstanding since the only classic circuits he knew at all before then were in Ulster and the Isle of Man.

In 1965, Honda equipped Ralph Bryans with a new four-stroke, twin-cylinder machine which was sufficiently fast and reliable to take the Irishman to the world title – the first, and so far (1977) the only, 50cc World Championship to be gained by Honda. Bryans won in Germany, France and Holland, and took the title by the narrow margin of four points from Honda's other lightweight rider, Luigi Taveri.

An intelligent, stylish, sensible rider, Ralph Bryans tucked himself neatly on to the small 50cc Honda and seldom travelled faster than was necessary to win a race. 'I only run when I know where the road goes,' he once said.

Between seasons Suzuki worked hard on their 50cc machines and a fine performance by Hans-Georg Anschiedt denied Bryans his second world title by just three points. Even so, Bryans could still have taken the title if Honda had not refused to compete in Japan, where they made a stand in defiance of what they believed to be the unacceptable dangers of the 3.7 mile Fisco circuit. The Irish rider's best performance that year was on the Isle of Man where he lapped the Mountain Circuit at 86.49mph and won the race at an average of 85.66mph. The lap speed was a new record and was to remain as such, no other rider on a similar capacity machine improving on the performance before the 50cc event was axed from the TT programme after 1968. He also took third place in the World Championship table in the 125cc class.

Bryans' championship career virtually ended when Honda sensationally withdrew from the 50cc World Championship at the end of 1966, though in 1967 he continued to race Hondas in the 250cc class, winning in Germany and Japan and finishing fourth in the table behind Hailwood, also on Honda, and Phil Read and Bill Ivy on Yamahas. PC

Above left: Ralph Bryans winds the howling six-cylinder Honda 250 round Gooseneck during the Isle of Man 250cc Lightweight TT of 1967

Far left: Ralph Bryans in action on the five-cylinder 125cc Honda at Oulton Park in 1968. Bryans was best known as a small bike rider and had already won the 50cc World Championship for Honda back in 1965

Florian Camathias

Right: Florian Camathias, ace rider, tuner and designer of racing sidecar outfits, pictured at Mallory Park in April 1965. Six months later he was back in Britain, racing at Brands Hatch in October, when his outfit left the road and he was killed

Below: Camathias and his passenger, Ducret, fly the Swiss flag on their helmets at Oulton Park on 19 April 1965, riding a 500cc BMW outfit with great style and the kind of speed which often embarrassed the factory teams

Far right: getting down to business on the Top Straight at Brands Hatch, with the Gilera four-cylinder engined machine which he campaigned (with little success) during 1964

ALTHOUGH HE NEVER won a world title, Florian Camathias was one of the two Swiss sidecar pilots who caused the German competitors so much trouble in the late 'fifties and early 'sixties. From 1954 until 1968, German machines monopolized the sidecar class and, not surprisingly, the best engines went to German riders. Florian, however, was not only a brilliant and consistent competitor he was also an ace tuner and respected designer. With his privately built and entered machines he was often the cause of much embarrassment to the BMW factory and their unofficial works teams. Along with compatriot Fritz Scheidegger, he threatened the German monopoly for many years.

Born in 1924, Florian was 31-years-old before he had the satisfaction of seeing his name on a Grand Prix result, with a fourth place at the 1955 Italian Grand Prix at Monza. The following year he finished fifth in the World Championship with a best placing of third at the Ulster GP, and in 1957 he finished third overall behind Hillebrand and Schneider. In 1958 he won his first Grand Prix in Holland and although he finished second in the other three Grands Prix (at the Isle of Man, Belgium and Germany) he was four points short of Schneider's total.

Whereas the German outfits were built with sidecars on the right of the bike, Camathias used a British style 'right hand drive' machine and with his privately prepared engines was a thorn in the flesh of the Munich factory. 1959 was the year when he came closest to winning the world title. He and Schneider both had two first places out of five races but the German had scored one more second place and took the title.

His passenger for the '59 season, Hilmar Cecco, was teamed up with another rider the following year, and in the three GPs in which he scored points, Camathias was partnered by three different passengers – one English, one Swiss, and one German, but even so the Swiss driver managed fourth place overall.

In 1961, Cecco was back with Camathias but during a meeting at Modena they crashed the outfit. Cecco was killed and Camantias sufficiently injured to be out of action for the rest of the season.

He returned in 1962 with Scheidegger's ex-passenger Burckardt and a new machine known as the Florian Camathias Special, which was still BMW powered. After swapping passengers once more he won the Belgian GP and was once more runner up in the World Championship.

In 1963 with yet another partner he won the German GP and the TT but was once more second to Deubel in the championship honours. The next season opened in Spain with Camathias winning on a new outfit powered by an old Gilera four-cylinder engine which had been lent by the Italian factory. The motor did not bring him success in any of the other rounds, however. While he finished fifteenth in the TT his friend Colin Seeley was second on the FCS.

Scheidegger broke the German monopoly by winning the Championship in '65 while Camathias was fourth. Sadly, while racing at Brands Hatch in October, his outfit left the road and the little Swiss, so popular with British crowds, was killed. However, despite the fact that he never gained the coveted World title, nor managed to fully wrest the domination of sidecar championships from Germany, he left a legacy of rugged determination and a host of creditable achievements on the international circuits. His efforts were palpable evidence that a privateer, with sufficient skill and perseverance, could provide serious competition for the factory backed teams fielded by BMW.   GE

Keith Campbell

Right: Australian Keith Campbell in action on his 350cc Manx Norton during an international race meeting held in Finland in 1955. Campbell won his class

Below: Campbell at speed on the fabulous V8 500cc Moto Guzzi during the 1957 Belgian Grand Prix at Spa. Mechanical failure forced Campbell to retire but not before he had set a new lap record

THE 350cc WORLD Championship won by Keith Campbell in 1957 was the last title to be won by a Guzzi-mounted rider and the first to be won by an Australian. That Campbell beat McIntyre and Liberati's Gileras after only two seasons of international racing suggests he had a natural talent for racing. His stay at the top, however, was only brief.

After showing early promise as a scrambles rider down under, he began to compete in road racing with a 350cc AJS. He came to Europe with an entry for the 1951 Manx Grand Prix but fell off on the mountain section of the course and sustained minor injuries. On his return to Australia, however, he put his European experience to good use and won several races and the 350cc Championship.

In 1955, he was back to contest the Continental Grand Prix races, but after taking part in a rider's

strike at the Dutch GP, he was banned by the FIM for six months, along with twelve other riders including Geoff Duke. The cause of the mass protest was the insufficient money offered to private entrants.

Ironically, that year saw the withdrawal of the British Norton and AJS works teams, but fortunately Keith was signed up to ride the works Guzzis in 1956. These machines were amongst the most specialised racing bikes ever seen. The 350cc and 250cc bikes were only singles, yet sophisticated wind tunnel testing, full dustbin fairings and space frame construction made them superior machines. For the 500cc class, Guzzi had developed the famous V8 – one of the most exotic machines ever raced.

In 1957, Campbell won the 350cc classes at the Belgian, Dutch, and Ulster Grands Prix, and in the Golden Jubilee TT he came home second, four minutes behind Bob McIntyre, but ahead of the second works Gilera and the MV Agusta of Surtees. In the Senior he finished fifth on a 500cc single behind the Gilera and MV fours and the Guzzi V8.

Although he never won a Grand Prix on the V8, Keith broke the lap record at Spa before retiring. Having won three of the six 350cc GPs and second in another, he took the World Championship from McIntyre and Liberati by 30 points to 22.

At the end of the season all the works teams withdrew from racing with the exception of MV Agusta. As a private entrant in 1958, Campbell could not hope to beat the Italian fours on his single-cylinder Nortons but he managed consistently good places in the early Grands Prix, finishing third behind the 350cc MVs of Surtees and Hartle at the Dutch and Belgian events. At the Belgian Spa circuit he also achieved the distinction of splitting the two works four-cylinder bikes by finishing second in the 500cc race behind Surtees.

Tragically, Campbell was killed later in the season at Cadours circuit during a 500cc race. He had made it to the top at a time when there was tough competition from other works teams, and even on inferior machinery had shown he could compete with some of the great riders of that time.   GE

Below: Keith Campbell on his way to fifth place on the 500cc single-cylinder Moto Guzzi in the Isle of Man Senior TT of 1957. He had been signed to ride for the famous Italian team a year before

Kel Carruthers

KEL CARRUTHERS WAS THE first rider to make his name on three continents, having won championship road races in Australia, Europe and the USA. Born in Australia in 1938, he took up road racing in the late 1950s riding his own Norton and Aermacchi machines, and later an ex-works Honda-4, loaned by the Honda distributors.

When he came to Europe in the 1960s he concentrated on the Grand Prix events and his first placing came in 1966 at Imatra in Finland, where he finished fourth on his 350cc Norton. The following year Kel rode his Norton to a few more places, and he also made the results on a 125cc production Honda. His best GP performance that year was at Belfast where he finished fourth in both 125 and 350 classes of the Ulster GP.

Although he was never a regular on the British short circuits, Kel was voted second behind Alan Barnett in the 1968 Grovewood Awards for private entrants on British circuits. He had also made a bigger impression on the Continental Circus that year with a 350cc Aermacchi, which had taken him to third place overall in the World Championship – the best Championship placing ever for the Italian factory.

Not surprisingly he made friends in Italy and for 1969 he was signed up by the Benelli factory to ride their 250-4s. With team-mate Pasolini, the Ossa-mounted Herrero and the Yamaha rider Kent Anderson to contend with, the season's Grands Prix were closely contested.

Carruthers' first win came at the TT, and was followed by second, third and fourth places until the Ulster where Kel was again the winner. By the time the last GP was held in Yugoslavia the title had not been decided, but by winning the race Kel took the title from Andersson.

Not content with being champion of the world, Carruthers went to America in 1970 to contest the Daytona 250cc race with a Don Vesco prepared Yamaha TD-2. He won the race first time out and then returned to Europe for the Grand Prix season. Although he won four GPs (one more than the previous season) he was beaten to the number one spot by Rod Gould. In the 350 class he was also second, this time behind the unbeatable MV of Agostini.

Ever the professional, Carruthers was impressed by what he had seen in the States, and in 1971 he quit the European scene to race Yamahas in the AMA series. In the 250 class Kel was supreme, winning six of the seven National races.

When Yamaha became involved in the bigger capacity superbike class, Kel's riding ability was surpassed by the new generation of American road racers, many of whom had been coached by the thorough-going Australian. However, much of the development work was being handled by Carruthers, and when he retired from racing in 1974, it was in order to run the Yamaha International race team, and in particular to look after the bikes of Grand National superstar Kenny Roberts. GE

Above left: Kel Carruthers (17) competing in the 1970 Lightweight TT at the Isle of Man. Following him are Santiago Herrero and Rod Gould and it was the latter who eventually won that year's 250cc World Championship

Far left: Carruthers at speed on his Yamaha TZ350 at Daytona. Carruthers was one of the first Europeans to recognise the potential of road racing in America. In 1971, he quit the European racing scene to settle in America and under his guidance and inspiration American road racers began to develop. Upon his retirement in 1974, Carruthers became a driving force within the American Yamaha team

Inset far left: 1969 250cc World Champion Kel Carruthers of Australia

John Cooper

JOHN COOPER WAS ONE of a generation of British riders who were prominent on the home circuits in the 1960s. Riding outdated machinery these 'privateers' were generally outclassed in Grand Prix races, yet were almost unbeatable on the British tracks. Cooper was one of the lucky ones who landed a works ride in the early 1970s when the British industry briefly revived the glamour of the factory teams.

He was born in Derby in 1938 and at the age of sixteen, John was riding a 197cc James. This was followed by more appropriate racing machinery with which he competed in club and national events, gaining the experience which took him to his first international win at Scarborough in 1961.

In those days everybody rode British four-stroke singles and for many years Cooper had the advantage of ace tuner Ray Petty's experience in fettling the 350 and 500cc Nortons. Although he raced with success at circuits all over the country, John was a critic of the TT, for which he considered the rewards inadequate, and he rarely raced abroad.

In 1964 he won the 350cc ACU Star and the following year he won the big race at his local circuit, the Mallory Park Race of the Year.

Above right: bespectacled John Cooper's trade mark was his famous 'mooneyes' helmet and an aggressive riding style that made him one of Britain's best known short-circuit 'scratchers'

Right: John Cooper in action aboard a works three-cylinder BSA 750 during the Transatlantic series meeting at Mallory Park in 1972

Far right top: Cooper takes part in a demonstration run on a Triumph at Brands Hatch in 1976

Centre right: John Cooper rounds Governors Bridge during the Senior TT at the Isle of Man in 1967

Far right centre: Cooper in action on the F750 John Player Norton during the Transatlantic series meeting at Brands Hatch in 1973

Far right bottom: Cooper 'wheelies' his BSA at Cadwell Park in 1972. A year earlier he had scored the most notable success of his career. At Mallory Park, mounted on the works 750cc BSA three, Cooper had won the Race of the Year event for the third time

In 1966 he was 350 and 500 British champion, the last honours he was to win with the Petty Nortons. Although he rode Seeleys for a while, Cooper also began to contest the smaller classes and in '68 became the 250cc British Champion. Realising the potential of the Yamaha motor, John and Colin Seeley developed the Yamsel, a potent 350 twin with which John won the Race of the Year for the second time in 1970, and many of the other races in which he rode it.

After being loaned a works BSA-3 for the 1971 Match Race series, Cooper contrived to work his way into the factory team. At last the rider with 'mooneyes' helmet had the machines and support he needed, and with it came his best season in fifteen years racing.

He beat Agostini's MV at Mallory to take the Race of the Year for a third time, and also beat him at Brands Hatch. In the same season he travelled to the United States for the first time where he won the 250-mile Classic at Ontario, California, with its handsome first prize cheque. Back at home he was voted Man of the Year.

Still on BSAs in 1972, John won the MCN

Superbike championship, but at the end of the season he signed for Norton. After crashing at Brands Hatch early in 1973, and breaking a leg, John Cooper retired from racing. At the end of nearly twenty years racing he had achieved his finest results on British machinery, and had become one of the leading figures in the new superbike class.

Although he was tempted to make a comeback John resisted. However, he still took an interest in the sport and helped John Newbold, among others, while running a garage in his home town. GE

Peter Craven

Below: Peter Craven holds off Barry Briggs during a meeting in June 1963

PETER CRAVEN'S NAME was written into the history books when he became only the second Englishman to win the world speedway title in 1955 and he became a double World Champion when he won again in 1962.

Tragedy, however, was just around the corner for the Belle Vue captain. On 20 September 1963, Belle Vue visited Edinburgh for a late season challenge match. In heat twelve, after riding to three wins, he lined up with Billy Powell against George Hunter and Willie Templeton. Craven was closely following Hunter when the Scotsman's bike seized up causing him to fall. Craven tried to avoid the fallen rider and crashed heavily. Craven was taken to hospital but died four days later from severe head injuries. All speedway mourned the death of the popular little champion. He was 29 years old.

The aptly titled 'master of balance' made the first of his ten World Final appearances in 1954. He scored only three points in that one which was one point more than another rider later to make a remarkable impression on the World Championship, Sweden's Ove Fundin.

Craven sprang to prominence by winning the world title the very next year in 1955, beating both the 1954 World Champion Ronnie Moore and Barry Briggs. He finished fourth in the world in 1956 despite blowing an engine and pushing home for third place after leading. He finished third in 1957, fourth in 1958, and scored seven points in 1959. The following year, 1960, saw an incredible three-man run-off for the title with Craven eventually finishing third.

Craven was second in the British Final at Wembley, but in the World Final at Malmo, Sweden, he fell in his first ride and scored only six points. 1962, however, was to be Craven's year again. He scored a brilliant fourteen points at Wembley to take the title outright.

For the ten years before his death, he was England's leading speedway ambassador. His career

began in Liverpool, his home town in 1951. It was his elder brother Brian who got him involved in speedway. As a youngster Craven had been involved with cycle speedway but in 1949, just after he turned sixteen, he used Brian's machine for a few laps at Stanley Park and sustained concussion after he hit the safety fence.

The eager young man practised on the Ainsdale sands but after one lap at Liverpool speedway he hit the safety fence again. Such were the beginnings of Craven's career. From those early, unsure steps, he went on to become a regular performer for England, captained his country, toured all over Europe, Russia and Poland and Australia. He was also a multi times winner of the famed Golden Helmet match race title, regularly beating Ove Fundin, Barry Briggs, Brian Crutcher and Ronnie Moore and many others.

A measure of Craven's great achievements can be best provided by one more statistic. It was another fourteen years before England had another world champion – this time another man with the initials PC, Peter Collins. It is certain that Craven could have given the world many more thrills.   AE

Above: Peter Craven (front row, right) at the semi finals of the 1962 World Championships held at Southampton

Below: Craven in action at Southampton

Dickie Dale

THROUGHOUT THE 1950s, road racing was dominated by the works teams of the Italian factories, and Dickie Dale was one of several English riders who were contracted to ride these exotic machines.

Dale first came to prominence when he won the Lightweight Manx GP of 1948 on a Moto Guzzi. A year later he returned to the Island as a member of the four man Guzzi team and was leading the 250 TT until he retired on the last lap with a failed engine. He stayed with Guzzi for four years and, although his racing successes were few, his talent for sorting out new machines was needed by the Italian factory.

In 1953, he joined the rival Gilera factory and rode their four-cylinder bikes alongside Duke, Milani, Liberati and Armstrong. He picked up a few places in the 500cc Grands Prix with a best result of second at the Italian round. The following year he was once more mounted on 500cc four-cylinder bikes but this time they were the MV machines of Count Agusta. After winning the final GP of the season in Spain, Dale finished fifth in the 500cc World Championship.

Dickie was back with the Guzzi team again in 1955 concentrating on the 350cc class. He won in Italy in front of the patriotic crowd and finished second to team mate Lomas in the Championship. In 1956 he tied with Hobl for second place in the 350 championship with Lomas once more taking the title.

With Guzzi campaigning their big V8 water-cooled 500 in 1957 the team travelled to the Isle of Man for the Golden Jubilee TT. Dale was leading the 350 race until he fell at Quarry Bends letting McIntyre through to win the first race of his famous double. In the Senior race Dickie took the dolphin-faired V8 to fourth place but further success did not follow and at the end of the season Guzzi withdrew from racing.

Most 500cc riders, apart from the MV team, were on private single-cylinder machinery for the 1958 season. Dale, however, was chosen to join Geoff Duke in the BMW team and after a tenth place in the TT he scored points in the other six Grands Prix to finish third in the 500cc World Championship behind the MVs. He also won the 'non-official' East German GP on the BMW, and raced an NSU in some 250cc races with a best place of sixth at the Ulster.

In 1959, he was once more teamed with Duke, this time to race the new machines from the Benelli factory who were making a return to GP racing. Sixth place in Sweden was his best result on the 250cc machines, although he had some success with his old BMW and also raced a 350cc AJS.

Dale joined the ranks of the 'privateers' for 1960, but his best performances on Nortons were spread over both 350 and 500 classes so he did not come close to the Championship leaders.

Although his racing career tended to be somewhat chequered, it encompassed a vast number of machines. Dale had ridden, with varying degrees of success, on BMWs, MV Agustas, MZs, AJSs, Gileras, Moto Guzzis, NSU and Norton, as well as having a brief foray with Benelli. Despite his lack of wins, his expertise in fathoming problems in new machines assured him of a position in the works teams. However it was as a privateer that he was killed at Nurburgring aboard a 250 MZ in 1961, robbing motor cycle sport of a colourful and competent rider. GE

Above: during his career, Dale rode for a number of famous teams, MV Agusta among them

Far left: Dale at speed on a four-cylinder MV Agusta. He spent 1954 riding for the legendary Italian team

Below left: Dale in action on the fabulous Moto Guzzi V8 Grand Prix racer of 1957

Harold Daniell

THERE WAS A time in the summer of 1938 when war with Hitler's Germany seemed very close and, in a surge of patriotism, a rather chunky, bespectacled, motor cycle dealer from North East London tried to enlist in the Military Police. 'Sorry', they said, 'your eyesight is much too poor.'

They were probably unaware that only a few weeks beforehand the hopeful applicant, Harold Daniell, had won the Senior TT on a works Norton, and in winning had become the first man to lap the Isle of Man course in under 25 minutes; his 91mph lap record was to remain unbroken until the coming of Geoff Duke and the immortal Featherbed Norton in 1950.

Harold's own career lasted into the days of the Featherbed, and at that same 1950 meeting he was to finish third in the Junior event. His career had begun away back in 1927, on miniature tracks such as Syston Park. By 1930 Harold had graduated to a 490cc CS1 overhead-camshaft Norton, and his exploits with this model in the early 1930s, particularly in the Manx Grand Prix series (where he was the 1933 Senior race winner) led to an offer to join the works AJS team.

For three years Harold persevered with AJS, his efforts including a frustrating 1936 Senior TT ride on the big blown vee-four, in air-cooled form, on which he worked up to ninth place, only to retire with supercharger-drive trouble. For all his efforts, his only win was in the 350cc class of the Leinster 100.

The following year he made the switch to Norton, although not as a fully-retained member of the Bracebridge Street brigade. Harold was on works machinery for the Dutch and German Grands Prix, but for other meetings he employed a rather special model, considerably lighter than standard, and highly tuned by his brother-in-law, the celebrated Steve Lancefield.

The Lancefield Norton won every British mainland race in which it was entered during the 1937 season (including in its successes wins at Crystal Palace, Donington Park and Brooklands) and took Harold to a highly creditable fifth place in the Senior TT, against opposition from quite a number of factory team riders.

It seemed at first as though Daniell might again have to rely on the Lancefield model for the 1938 Senior TT. This time he had been entered by the factory, but the official machines were a long time coming, and so Harold had to use the private bike for the earlier practice sessions.

A slide at Ballacraine landed him in hospital for a few days, and though he was out again in time for race week, his hospitalisation meant that he had had only one practice outing on the works machine. Understandably, then, it took him a little while to get going, and not until the closing stages did he make his presence felt. On the fifth of the seven laps he equalled the existing lap record, on the last he shattered it, to run home as winner by fifteen seconds from Stanley Woods riding a Velocette.

Daniell had certainly shown himself to be a tough character, and he was to prove it yet again in 1950, right at the end of his motor cycling career, when he came to the TT with his hand in plaster, a souvenir of a Silverstone crash in which he broke a bone. He pleaded with the doctor to be given a bit more movement, and so the plaster was chipped away and, instead, a newly-devised plastic appliance substituted. The outcome was third place in the Junior event and fifth in the Senior. They were pretty good results for a bloke with poor eyesight! FG

Above: Harold Daniell's 'poor' eyesight may have kept him out of the military police but it proved to be no handicap on a motor cycle and he became one of the sport's best known figures

Right: Daniell was one of that rare breed of riders who stuck faithfully to one marque for many years, establishing and maintaining his superiority with Nortons between 1937 and 1949. His last major victory came in the 1949 Senior TT, just a year before he 'retired' to the motor cycle trade

Far right: posing on his Norton after taking his classic victory in the 1938 Senior TT. In the course of beating Stanley Woods' Velocette into second place, Daniell became the first rider to lap the Island in under 25 minutes. Daniell was loyal to Norton throughout his career

Ernst Degner

BORN IN Germany in 1931, Ernst Degner was one of the team who developed the MZ rotary valve two-stroke, an East German machine which became the first world class two-stroke racer.

The first big success for the East Germans came in 1957 when Degner won the 125 race at the non-official East German Grand Prix, and also made his way into the results on the other side of the iron

curtain at the West German Grand Prix, where he finished sixth and his team mate Fugner finished in fourth position.

The MZ team was sent to the Isle of Man in 1958, and Degner and Fugner finished fifth and sixth in the 125 race. A full season of Grands Prix followed with several good results for Ernst, including a third place at Nürburgring, where other MZ riders also took the next three places.

In 1959 Degner finished fifth in the 125cc World Championship and fourth in the 250 class. In the last Grand Prix of the season, at Monza, Ernst won the 125cc race, which was his first championship Grand Prix victory.

The next season saw Degner finish third in the 125 Championship behind the works MVs and ahead of the new Hondas The East German factory concentrated on the 125 class again in 1961 when they were up against the full Honda team of Phillis, Taveri and Redman. Degner and Phillis were involved in some very close racing all season with Phillis taking the early points lead, although Degner had won both East and West German Grands Prix. There were now eleven Grands Prix in the calendar instead of the previous season's five and by the penultimate round, in Sweden, Degner was on top of the points table.

At this crucial stage in his career Degner surprised the racing world by defecting to the west. Had he raced in Sweden and beaten Phillis he would

have been champion, but the Honda rider came home sixth leaving the last round in Buenos Aires as the deciding race. Degner started the race on an English EMC, a machine which closely resembled the MZ. However, the bike failed and Phillis won the race and picked up the title.

As a member of the Suzuki team in 1962 Degner competed in the new 50cc class. He won the TT and the next three Grands Prix, then missed out the East German round before clinching the World Championship with second and fourth places in the last two Grands Prix.

Although Suzuki repeated the 50cc win and also took the 125cc title in 1963, Degner only managed a third in the 50cc Championship behind team leader and multiple champion Hugh Anderson. After crashing at the last round in Japan, Ernst was badly burned and he did not regain his form until the end of the next season when a third place at Monza was followed by a convincing win on his return to Suzuki's home base in Japan.

In 1965 Degner went to Daytona where he won the 50cc race; he went on to win again at Spa, although he only made fourth place in both 50 and 125 championships. His last Grand Prix win came on the 125 at Ulster where he beat the two works MZs into second and third places.

Although he had officially retired at the end of 1965, Ernst returned to the Isle of Man in 1966 for the last 50cc TT, which he finished in fourth place. GE

Far left top: Degner in action on the works MZ during 1957

Above left: Ernst Degner was both a top class Grand Prix racer and a top rate development engineer. He was an East German, but he defected to the West in 1962

Left bottom: apart from his contracts with MZ and Suzuki, Degner also rode for a small English team, EMC. He was always at his best on two-stroke machines and had a first class knowledge in modifying such machines

Above: Ernst Degner joined the Suzuki team in time for the 1962 season and went on to win the 50 cc World Championship title for the factory

Max Deubel

MAX DEUBEL was the most consistent sidecar road racer of the sixties, and only the second man to win the World Championship four times, which he did in consecutive years from 1961–1964. Like every other top Grand Prix sidecar team at that time, Deubel and passenger Emil Horner were BMW mounted. Their first World Championship points were scored at the West German Grand Prix of 1959 when they finished in a fighting third place.

1960 was the year of fellow German Helmut Fath, but Max gained experience in his first full Grand Prix season and finished the year with points from two fourth and one sixth place. Fath was out of action soon after the start of the 1961 season, and Max became the official BMW entry.

With the advantage of a works engine and the additional absence of Camathias, Deubel's only competition came from Scheidegger. By the last round at Spa, Deubel and Horner had won three Grands Prix while Scheidegger had won only once, yet had three second places to his credit. In the final race Max came home second behind the Swiss team, but he had scored well enough to win the Championship by the narrow margin of only two points.

The partnership began the 1962 season with two outright wins, and when they arrived at the Isle of Man they were TT favourites. They got off to a record breaking start with the first 90mph sidecar lap of the Mountain circuit, but crashed on the second lap and allowed Chris Vincent's BSA through as the first non-BMW Grand Prix winner for five years.

Second and third places at the Dutch and Belgian rounds were followed by another victory at the last round in Germany, where Deubel clinched his second title in front of his home crowd.

In 1963 the three-cornered fight between the official BMW team and the two Swiss riders, Camathias and Scheidegger, continued. Although Deubel only won two GPs, his two second places guaranteed his third title by the slender margin of two points over both the challengers.

The consistency of the Deubel/Horner partnership brought them points in all six Grands Prix in 1964, including maximum points for winning the TT. Once more it was a close contest with Max again beating Scheidegger by two points to take his fourth World Championship, and equal the record set by Eric Oliver in the fifties.

He won the TT for the third time in 1965 but did not score in three Grands Prix. The positions were reversed and Max was beaten into second place in the championship by his great rival Scheidegger.

Deubel's consistency returned in the 1966 season when he finished second four times and third once out of five GPs but, unfortunately for him, Scheidegger had come home first in every one of those races. The TT saw one of the most dramatic finishes with Deubel only eight tenths of a second behind at the end of a spectacular race.

After two seasons in second place the team broke up; Deubel to manage his hotel, and Horner to return to his trade of mechanic.   GE

Above right: Max Deubel, World Champion sidecar racer from 1961 to 1964

Right: Max Deubel and Emil Horner in action on their 500 BMW at Brands Hatch in 1966

Above right: Deubel 'opposite locks' his BMW during the Sidecar TT Isle of Man of 1965. Deubel went on to win the race, the third time he had taken victory in a TT event

Far right top: Max Deubel (right) enjoys a joke with his passenger Emil Horner. Deubel and Horner worked together from their first championship race in 1959 until their retirement at the end of 1967

Far right bottom: the Deubel/ Horner BMW 500 at speed at Oulton Park in 1965

Freddie Dixon

IN ALL THE annals of TT history, only one man has ever won the laurels on two, three, and four wheels – even if that last claim is stretching a point, because the event was run off in Northern Ireland rather than the Isle of Man. That man was Freddie Dixon, a rip-roarin', devil-may-care character whose epitaph could well have read I Did It My Way.

Far right: Dixon (Indian) at the 1922 Senior TT

Below: Freddie Dixon with the Harley-Davidson sidecar at Brooklands, 1921

Known as the 'Wild Man of the North', Fred cared little for the conventions. He had never worn goggles when racing, and when at last the regulations were re-written to make eye protection compulsory, he came to the line wearing goggles from which he had removed the lenses. Nobody said a word.

His bikes had always to be specially tailored in the American style, even to footboards instead of footpegs, a twistgrip instead of lever throttle, and a foot-operated clutch. That, however, was a legacy of his early experience of Indian and (especially) eight-valve Harley-Davidson track models.

Talking of Harleys, did you hear about the time Dixon was due to ride a works twin in a Brooklands 500-Mile Race? Unknown to Fred, the machine had been set up wrongly, with sidecar instead of solo steering geometry, and during practice he found it hard to stay in the saddle.

Smitten by a bright idea, he stuck a sheet of emery cloth to the seat, rough side up. But before the race was a hundred miles old he had the feeling that all was not well and, groping around behind, he found his glove smeared with blood. The emery had worn right through his leathers, and was starting to attack his posterior. At a hasty pit-stop, he wrenched away the emery cloth and restarted.

But that wasn't the end of his troubles. A little while later the front tyre came off the rim when he was touching 90mph, and he did half a dozen somersaults. He ran back to the machine, edged the tyre back into place, trickled round to the pits, fitted a new cover – and raced on, to finish second.

That was Freddie all over, the toughest cookie that ever was. His first TT race, on a Middlesborough-built Cleveland-Precision, was as far back as 1912, but a faulty magneto meant that he didn't make instant headlines. Those came later when, after World War I army service, he set up in business in Middlesborough as a motor cycle dealer, holding the Harley-Davidson franchise.

His first Isle of Man victory was the 1923 Sidecar TT, in which Fred drove a Douglas outfit equipped with a banking sidecar of his own design; a long lever, operated by the passenger, lowered or raised the outfit's sidecar wheel for left- or right-hand bends respectively.

The device worked fine, even if the chassis did collapse near the end of the race, so that he finished with the chair leaning against the bike in loving proximity. Self-taught, perhaps, but Dixon turned out to be a brilliant engineer, and his services were employed by the Douglas company in designing and developing their road-going models. Later, he was to be involved with George Brough in the design of the flat-four Golden Dream, a machine which, alas, the coming of World War II meant would never be produced. Later still, Douglas called him back to lend a helping hand in sorting out the post-war transverse twins.

In the 1930s, however, he began to carve out a new career as a car racer, with a home-tuned Riley that ran rings round the official factory jobs. The secret? Under the car's bonnet (which he kept padlocked) lived a bank of Amal motor cycle carburettors, one to each pot. The rest was just painstaking preparation and sheer hard work.

But if Freddie Dixon rode hard, when the race was over he played hard, too, as many a continental café or casino owner knew only too well. There was one race meeting (the 1921 Belgian Grand Prix, at Spa) of which the aftermath is still a part of motor cycle racing legend. On an Indian, Fred finished third – and, possibly foolishly, the local FN armaments firm presented pistols of their own make to the leading bunch, by way of souvenirs. Wouldn't you know that Dixon would decide on target practice, leaving the headquarters hotel with as many little perforations as a tea-bag?   FG

Helmut Fath

THE SUCCESS STORY of German sidecar racer Helmut Fath is unparalleled in any form of motor cycle sport. After winning a world title for BMW he was sidelined for a couple of years with injuries, but returned to racing with an engine of his own design and, eight years later, carried off another title.

Fath achieved international success in 1958 when he finished third in his first World Championship season. The following year he finished fifth overall but World Champion Walter Schneider retired at the end of the season and in 1960 Fath challenged for the title.

In an outstanding season he and passenger Alfred Wohlgemuth were winners of four of the five Grands Prix, and finished second in the fifth. They had scooped up the World Championship title by a margin of eight points. Among the lap records they set was one of 85.79mph at the TT.

1961 started well for the German pair with a win at the opening Grand Prix in Barcelona. However, they crashed at a non-championship meeting at Nürburgring and Wohlgemuth was killed. Fath's own injuries were enough to put him out of racing for several seasons.

He planned to return in 1963 but BMW, who were sponsoring Max Deubel, would not provide the engine Helmut wanted. Determined to return with competitive machinery, Fath set about designing and building his own world-beating engine with the technical assistance of Dr Peter Kuhn.

The four-cylinder, fuel injection, dohc 500cc motor was running two years later, and in 1967 Fath was back on the Grand Prix circuits, although mechanical problems kept him out of the results.

The 1968 season opened with a shock for the BMW factory. At the first Grand Prix, in Germany, all the BMWs were beaten by Fath on his URS machine, named after his home of Ursenback. In the next three races he could manage no more than one fourth and one fifth place. But he won the last two

Grands Prix of the season and became World Champion for the second time, and in so doing broke BMW's fourteen year monopoly of the title.

His feat was applauded by enthusiasts everywhere, and in England he was voted MCN Man of the Year – only the second foreigner and the first sidecar pilot to win that honour. After five of the 1969 Grands Prix, Helmut was once again leading the championship chase with three wins to his credit. However, he crashed in the penultimate Finnish round and missed the last Grand Prix, both of which were won by Klaus Enders who became the new World Champion.

Fath's enforced retirement at the end of the season let BMW rider Enders through to a second consecutive title, but in 1971 the name of Fath was back at the top of the sidecar World Championship.

His outfit, now known as the URS-Fath, was taken to a surprise championship victory by Horst Owesle, an associate of Fath who had worked on the development of the machine. This second title proved to the world – and the mighty BMW company – that Fath's design and engineering skills were as great as his riding ability. GE

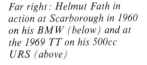

Far right: Helmut Fath in action at Scarborough in 1960 on his BMW (below) and at the 1969 TT on his 500cc URS (above)

Below: Helmut Fath and his URS opposite-locking their way round Mallory Park

Bob Foster

THEY CALLED HIM 'Fearless Foster', and with good reason. After all, few others would have been brave enough to hurl a dope-burning ex-works New Imperial twin at the 1-in-1 slope of Red Marley freak hill climb; still fewer could have wrestled that super-charged, water-cooled camel, the V4 AJS, around the Ulster Grand Prix course. For that matter, not many would have gone scrambling or grass-tracking on a big 600cc, single-cylinder Levis.

Most enthusiasts think of Albert Robert Foster as a road racer – and indeed he was, with two TT wins, and the 1950 350cc World Championship to his credit. But he was actually an all-rounder who qualified for the British Experts Trial each year from 1931 to 1939, represented Britain in the 1946 Moto-Cross des Nations squad, and was pre-war Western Centre grass track champion.

A Gloucestershire lad of farming stock, Bob Foster began on the grass tracks, but in 1932 he travelled to the Isle of Man as mechanic for a pal competing in the Manx Grand Prix. The bug bit, he bought a 350cc Grand Prix New Imperial of his own, and began to go places to such good effect that the works sat up and took notice.

At first they provided spares, but in 1934 they went further, lending him a works 250cc racer for the Manx Grand Prix. He should have won, too, except that when his pit hung out a 'take it easy' signal, he slowed too much and was relegated to second.

Bob's final excursion for the New Imperial factory was in the 1936 250cc TT, the last-ever win by a Briton on a British-made bike in that class. Un-happily, the works was running into financial trouble and, immediately after the race, they announced their withdrawal from racing, leaving Bob to ride as a privateer for the rest of the season.

However, AJS were in need of a jockey for their potent but unpredictable vee-four, and Bob campaigned this machine up to the outbreak of World War II. With the resumption of racing in 1946 he tried a Triumph, followed by the wide-angle 500cc Moto-Guzzi twin and, in the 350cc class, a works Velocette.

The Velo brought him his second TT victory, in the 1947 Junior race, and, three years later, his World Championship title. However, the war period had robbed Bob Foster of what should have been his peak years and, already, a new breed of racing men was arising. His 1950 Championship had been gained by the narrowest of margins from one of these up-and-coming youngsters, one Geoff Duke. Time, thought Bob, to pack it in.

Still, the Velocette works had devised a new 250cc, and Foster was tempted back for just one more season, to ride both this and the 350cc model. He was on the three-fifty for his last race of all, the Ulster Grand Prix. Typically, he gave it all he had and was dicing furiously with Reg Armstrong (AJS) when the Velo engine cried 'enough'. It was a dull note on which to end a distinguished career.   FG

Far right: Bob Foster seen on the large Moto Guzzi 500cc machine at the 1949 TT. Although he set the fastest lap he retired with mechanical trouble

Right: Bob Foster, riding a 350cc Velocette in the 1947 Junior TT, takes the chequered flag for his second win in the event. He is seen celebrating with his son soon after

Rem Fowler

Above: H. Rem Fowler poses on the Peugeot-engined Norton on which he won the twin-cylinder class at the first Isle of Man TT races back in 1907. Rem's winning speed was 36.22 mph, but this included a couple of punctures and a fall

Far right: Rem Fowler (2), aboard a vee-twin Norton, awaits the start of the 1908 TT. Alongside him are Charlie Collier (1) and Harry Collier (3). Pictured inset is Fowler in his later years with the vee-twin 1907 Norton

AT VARIOUS TIMES in the 1950s or '60s, a visitor to the finishing enclosure at the Isle of Man TT might have seen an elderly gentleman, in deerstalker cap and (latterly) leaning heavily on a stick, offering a congratulatory word or two to Mike Hailwood and, probably, nibbling a piece of Mike's birthday cake.

Not only did Harry Rembrant Fowler share the same birthday as Hailwood, however, he and Mike both appeared in the list of TT winners, even though a considerable number of years separated the two entries. Rem, in fact, was the winner of the twin-cylinder class at the first TT meeting of all, back in the year of 1907.

Even that wasn't his first venture into the competition world, because he had been taking part in Birmingham MCC hill-climbs, on a Rex, for several months beforehand. It was at one such climb (Rose Hill, Rednal) that he first made the acquaintance of James L. Norton, at that time in a very small way of business in Floodgate Street, Birmingham, and decided to buy a Peugeot-engined vee-twin 5hp Norton for the new Tourist Trophy races which were to be held in the Isle of Man.

There was nothing 'works-supported' about it. Rem paid for the machine, every penny of it, out of his own pocket. And although the manufacturer, James Norton himself, agreed to accompany Rem to the Isle of Man and act as his pit attendant, it was on the understanding that Rem would pay half the expenses involved.

For that 1907 event, the course was not as used now. Instead, it started at St John's green, alongside Tynwald Mount, and ran to Ballacraine,

where it joined the present route until the outskirts of Kirkmichael were reached. It then swung back along the coast road to Peel, and so again to St John's. The lap was just short of sixteen miles, and it had to be covered ten times.

Rem's winning twin-cylinder speed was a modest 36.22mph, but his was an adventurous ride which included a fall and a couple of punctures. On one occasion, recalled Rem in later years, Mr Norton thrust out a piece of board on which he had chalked the word 'Oil'; his sensitive ear had told him the engine was running dry, and this was a reminder to the rider to operate the hand oil pump. It was surely the first pit signal in history!

Rem Fowler competed in the Isle of Man for several more years, but he was never again to hit the headlines. After an unsuccessful attempt in 1908 on the Norton vee-twin, he reverted to Rex machines for the 1909 and 1910 events, finishing sixteenth each time. Finally, when the full mountain circuit was brought into use for the first time in 1911, he switched to a New Hudson for the Junior race, and an Ariel for the Senior.

Thereafter he dropped out of active competition, but he retained his interest in the sport right through to an advanced old age. A toolmaker by trade, he was still working, and driving himself around in a little Morris, in his late 80s. And there was nothing he liked better, than to drop in at a Vintage MCC clubnight for a natter about the times that were. Truly, he was the Grand Old Man of motor cycling and his name will live on in the memories of motor cycle enthusiasts. FG

Freddie Frith

TO THE MAN in the street, it might have seemed that in 1949 Freddie Frith was at his road-racing peak. After all, he had just won (on a Velocette) the World 350cc Road Racing Championship, and hadn't he been honoured by the award of the OBE in consequence, the first time any motor cyclist had received such recognition of his services?

Yet there was Freddie, folding his leathers for the last time, hanging up his helmet, waving goodbye to the racing circuits and, instead, throwing all his effort into opening a motor cycle shop in Grimsby. That's right; Grimsby, of all places, an unfashionable fishing port on the east coast of England.

Frith did have reason enough for packing up the racing game. He realised, even if the fans didn't, that he was already forty years old, that the clock was galloping on and that he had really been at his best in the late 1930s. Among his many victories was a win in the Junior TT of 1936 (his first TT win) which he followed with a win in the 500cc Ulster Grand Prix. During the following year, 1937, he also achieved his ambition of winning the Senior TT, clocking up the race's first ever over 90mph lap. The world crown should have been his in 1938, or maybe 1939, but by then the rumbles of war were already being heard and Norton, the team for which he was then riding, had brought development of racing machines to a halt.

Then came the six year pause and, thereafter, things were never the same. True, there were other racers – Bob Foster and Harold Daniell, for example – whose track careers had suffered similarly; but, also, a new breed of youngsters was already on the way, ready to take over from the established kings. Yes, it was time to step down. Still, he had won the Junior TT of 1948 and the 350cc Ulster Grand Prix as well as his famous challenge on the 1949 world 350cc title.

As for Grimsby . . . well, why not? It was the town where he had been born and raised and where, when not racing, he had earned his living as a stonemason. Besides, Freddie could foresee the day when the South Humberside area would be a boom area, as more and more new factories came into being. Factories meant workers. Workers needed transport.

All the same, watchers from the trackside would certainly be the losers by Frith's retirement, for his was possibly the neatest riding style of any. Chin pressed down into the tank-top sponge pad, knees tucked well in to the machine's flanks, backside hovering over the rear of the seat, he was the classic racing man of the 'thirties personified.

Far right: Frith and the Velocette at the Ulster Grand Prix of 1947

Below: Freddie Frith (Norton) at the Senior TT of 1938. The race was won by fellow Norton rider Harold Daniell at a speed of 89.11mph

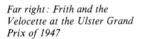

Yet that riding style really happened along by accident – quite literally so. His first true road race was the 1930 Junior Manx Grand Prix, run off in a heavy rainstorm, and for it Fred had a camshaft Velocette. In the soaking conditions he dropped the bike a couple of times, finishing with one end of the handlebar up and the other bent down.

Two days later came the Senior Manx, in which he was due to ride the same 350cc Velocette. Smitten with a bright idea, he bent the other end of the handlebar downwards to match that damaged in his spills, and the outcome was a streamlined riding position. Others copied him, and soon nobody was trying to race while sitting on the saddle any more. Thus heralding clip-on bars right back in 1930.

If Freddie Frith's riding style was immaculate, then so were his machines. It was his philosophy that the rider with a spotless machine starts the race with that little extra degree of confidence in his machinery and himself. It's a creed that many a modern racer could take to heart.   FG

Rod Gould

RODNEY GOULD began his racing career in the early 'sixties on a BSA Gold Star, but by 1964 the 20-year-old Banbury rider was campaigning the traditional brace of 350 and 500 Nortons on the British circuits. By the end of the decade he had become a top line international rider on two-stroke Yamaha machines.

He began riding the Japanese lightweights in 1967, although that year also saw Gould's first placing in a 500cc Grand Prix when he finished fifth on his Norton at the East German GP. The following year at the first GP of the season, at Nürburgring, he finished sixth on the big single, and came home fourth on his 250 Yamaha. In his first full season on the 'Continental Circus' Rod performed consistently well. Three third places, three fourth places and two fifth spots took him to fourth place overall in the hotly contested 250 championship. His performances on the home circuits in 1968 also earned him third place in the Grovewood Awards for non-works riders.

In 1969 Gould was supplied with free machines by Yamaha as part of their semi-works participation, but that year his best performances came on the 350 bike with which he finished fifth in the table. His results in that class had included second places behind Ago's MV in three consecutive Grands Prix. Rod's appearances at non-championship meetings that year included a visit to the new Swedish circuit at Anderstorp where he won the inaugural race for production bikes.

The next year, 1970, was Rod Gould's most outstanding season. With riders like 1969 champion Kel Carruthers, second place man Kent Andersson, multiple champion Phil Read and Jarno Saarinen riding similar 250cc TD-2 production racers, and the

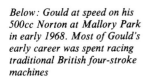

Below: Gould at speed on his 500cc Norton at Mallory Park in early 1968. Most of Gould's early career was spent racing traditional British four-stroke machines

Far right: in 1970 Rod Gould became World 250cc Champion. He is seen here at the non-championship Hutchinson 100 meeting at Brands Hatch on his Yamaha

works machines from MZ and Ossa all in contention, the season did not start too well for Rodney. By mid season however, he had taken over the points lead, and he steamed away to win the title by eighteen points from Carruthers. He had won six of the twelve Grands Prix, and finished second twice.

Read was trying hard again in 1971, and it was not until the eighth Grand Prix of the season that

Gould scored a 250 win. The meeting was the first official Swedish GP and was run at Anderstorp where Rod had already shown his mastery. He won again in Finland and picked up more points in Ulster and Italy. At the last race of the season, however, Read finished second with Rod nowhere in sight. He had missed his second title by just five points.

In 1972 Gould won the 250 Dutch TT and again proved invincible in Sweden, where he also finished second to Ago in the 500cc race. Even his consistent record of second, third and fourth places in the other races only gained enough points for Gould to finish third overall.

At the end of the season Rod retired from competition to run the Amsterdam based Yamaha racing operation.   GE

Below: Rod Gould in action at Mallory Park in 1968 on a 250cc Yamaha two-stroke twin. Gould started riding the Japanese machines in 1967 and is still associated with the company today

Les & Stuart Graham

WHEN THE road racing World Championships were introduced in 1949, the first 500cc champion was an Englishman – Les Graham, riding an English machine, an AJS.

Les was a leading rider on the British circuits before the war interrupted his motor cycling activities. After distinguished service as a bomber pilot he returned in 1947 to lead the AJS works team. In the Senior TT of that year Les rode the famous Porcupine machine which he had to push across the line to finish in ninth place. Two years later he was leading the race on an improved version of the same bike when it broke down on the last lap. Although the Porcupine was out of luck on the Island, Les won the Swiss and Ulster GPs and carried off the title by a single point only.

In 1950, still riding Ajays, he finished fourth in the Senior TT and third overall in both 250 and 500 championships. His 350 mount for 1951 was a Velocette with which Les won the Swiss GP and came second in Spain, but during that year he was signed up by MV Agusta to develop and race their new four-cylinder bike. Les was a respected development rider and in 1952 he took the 'four' to its first GP wins in Italy and Spain, and finished the season in second place. He was also fourth on an MV in the 125 championship, and third in the 250 class on a Velocette machine.

In 1953 Les, who was a great favourite with the crowds, won his first TT, on the 125 MV. The next day, however, while lying second to Duke in the Senior, he crashed heavily at Bray Hill and the great rider was killed.

Below: Les Graham (right) in action on his works AJS during the 1950 Isle of Man Senior TT. He eventually finished in fourth place

A decade later the name of Graham was once again in the race results as Les's son Stuart began to make his mark with 350 AJS and 500 Matchless machines. In 1966 Stuart was contesting the Grands Prix in the 500cc class where his best result was a second place to Agostini's MV at Spa. The young Graham was also offered a works ride by Honda who entered him on the six-cylinder 250. His best results on this exotic bike were two second places behind Hailwood, one of which was on the Isle of Man, the other in Finland. Signed up by Suzuki for the 1967 season, Stuart rode in the 125cc and 50cc classes. He finished third in the 125 World Championship behind Ivy and Read, after a second place in the TT, a win in Finland and several other good rides.

In the 50cc class he also finished third overall behind team mates Anscheidt and Katayama. At his last Grand Prix as a Suzuki teamster in Japan he finished second in both small classes, but his most satisfactory result had come about earlier in the year when he won the 50cc TT.

Fourteen years after his father's one and only TT victory, Stuart had brought the Graham name back to the list of TT winners.   GE

Above: Stuart Graham, son of Les, at Cadwell Park on his AJS in 1964 and (below) at Oulton Park in 1968 on the incredible works two-stroke 125cc Suzuki from Japan

Jimmy Guthrie

JIMMY GUTHRIE was one of the great names of the early days of motor cycling. His reputation as a rider and sportsman will ensure that he remains one of motor cycle sport's all time legends. He is also a pioneer among Scottish sporting heroes.

Born in 1897 in Hawick, Scotland, Guthrie rode motor cycles all over Britain in his early twenties, racing at speed trials and at circuits such as Brooklands. In 1923 he paid his first visit to the Isle of Man, where he was later to do so well. His first outing, however, in the Junior race of that year ended inauspiciously for Jimmy – he retired with engine problems on his Matchless.

He did not return to the Island until 1927, riding a New Hudson in the Senior race. He finished second to Alec Bennett's works Norton. Guthrie raced only occasionally on the mainland over the next two years with little success, but in 1930 he had more luck.

Having already won the 350cc German Grand Prix, Jimmy was entered in the Lightweight TT on a new works 250cc AJS machine. He won the race, although surprisingly the 250cc AJS was never raced again.

In 1931 Guthrie moved to the Norton team to ride their new machines with redesigned overhead camshafts, an engine design which lasted with steady development for thirty years. He finished second in the Senior race, a result which he repeated the fol-

lowing year. In 1933 he was third in the Junior and fourth in the Senior, both of which were won by Stanley Woods.

Although he had been performing well at other circuits, Jimmy Guthrie's best year on the Island was not until 1934 when he became only the third man to do the double by winning the Senior and Junior races. In 1935, he almost thought he had done it again when cheered in by the crowds after the 500cc race, only to find that Woods had avoided a pit stop and brought his Moto Guzzi in four seconds ahead of the Scot.

The same year Jimmy won the Swiss and German Grands Prix, and established a new world one hour record of 114.092mph at the high-speed Montlhéry circuit in France.

He won the Swiss and German races again in 1936 and beat Woods by eight seconds in the Senior TT. In the Junior he had been relegated to fifth place with chain trouble.

He was now European champion and looked set to sweep the Grands Prix again in 1937. He won the Swiss for a third time, and although retiring in the Senior TT, scored a superb victory for the Norton team in the Isle of Man in Junior race.

Six weeks later, however, while leading the 500cc race at Sachsenring, he crashed on the last lap and was killed. Jimmy Guthrie was forty years of age and seemingly at his peak as a racer.

The British enthusiasts had lost a hero, and two years later they honoured him when the Guthrie Memorial was unveiled between the Gooseneck and the Mountain Mile.   GE

Far right: Guthrie poses on the works Norton. Guthrie joined the Norton team in 1931. Before that he had ridden, among others, New Hudson and AJS machines

Below right: Jimmy Guthrie was one of the most famous of British pre-World War II motor cycle riders

Above: Jimmy Guthrie at speed on the works Norton record breaker at the famous circuit at Montlhéry in France in 1935

Right: Guthrie in action on the works Norton during his victorious ride in the Isle of Man Junior TT of 1935. In the Senior TT, he was beaten to the winning post by Stanley Woods' Guzzi by only four seconds

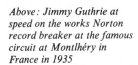

Werner Haas

WHEN THE young German road racer Werner Haas won the 125cc race at Solitude during the 1952 German GP, he was beginning a very rapid rise to a brief period of stardom. In only two full seasons of Grand Prix racing Haas won three world championships, and then retired from the sport.

His early rides had been on a 125cc Puch, but in 1952 the German NSU factory chose Werner to ride their new 123cc single, and 248cc twin-cylinder racers. The Solitude victory was the first Grand Prix success for NSU, but it was also the last for that season. In the final championship meeting of the year at Monza, Haas demonstrated the potential of the double overhead cam 250 twin by finishing second to champion Lorenzetti's Guzzi.

The first race on the 1953 calendar was the TT and Haas, who had never seen the Island before, obviously found the circuit to his liking. He came home second in the 125cc race behind Les Graham's MV, and finished the 250 race in the same spot, just seventeen seconds behind the Guzzi of Fergus Anderson. At the next Grand Prix, in Holland, Haas beat the might of the MV and Guzzi teams to win both races. His consistency in both classes and the obvious superiority of the new NSUs, saw the newcomer walk off with two world championships in only his first full year of international competition.

Haas became the first German to win a world title, and was only the second man to achieve a championship double. In the smaller class he was ten points ahead of the nearest MV, while his success on the 250 machine was backed up by team mate Reg Armstrong who was only five points behind in second place.

In 1954 Werner won the first five 250 Grands Prix outright, on a re-designed 250 machine, which now had a claimed output of 42bhp – as much as the 350s of 1961. The unit construction engines featured a modified camshaft drive and were mated to six speed gear boxes, yet the frames and cycle parts were almost identical to the roadster 'Max'. The racers of 1954 did, however, carry unorthodox 'dolphin' fairings with the characteristic 'beak' projecting over the exposed front wheel.

On the Isle of Man, Haas pushed the race average to over 90mph, a good 4mph faster than the previous year, and four out of the next five places were also taken by his team mates in this show of NSU strength. Appropriately the fifth of those GPs, at which Haas clinched his third title, was the German round at Solitude which he won in a record time which was faster than the 350 race time...

Obviously satisfied that their point had been made, the NSU factory closed down the race shop at the end of 1954, having collected four championships in two years. Although Haas was undoubtedly a skilled rider all his international experience had been on these phenomenal machines. When the team disbanded, Werner hung up his leathers after what had been a brief but spectacular career. Sadly, he was killed in an air crash in the spring of 1955.   GE

Below: Werner Haas on his way to winning the 250cc Dutch Grand Prix on his works NSU in 1953. He went on to win both the 125 and 250cc World Championships for the German NSU team. He repeated this achievement again the following year, after which NSU withdrew from Grand Prix racing

Right: Haas in action on the 1953 NSU Rennmax

Far right: in 1954, Werner Haas again won the 250cc world title using this streamlined NSU

Torsten Hallman

Right: the forceful Hallman on his 250 Husqvarna during the British Grand Prix of 1968. Hallman was, for fifteen years, a development rider for Husqvarna and the company owed much of its success to his skill and ability

TORSTEN HALLMAN probably has more right to the title of 'Mr Motocross' than anyone else in the sport in the last two decades. It is, in any case, the title of his autobiography which still stands as one of the best records of a motor cycle sportsman. But it probably wasn't his choice.

The shy Swede has never been one to shout about his achievements, even though he has far more to boast about than most. Quiet, polite and sociable, he has none of the imposing air of a superstar. Yet twenty years on he is still making a significant impact on the sport which has made his fame and his fortune.

Through one of those ironies of history, Hallman, the man who led the two-stroke invasion of motocross with four World Championships in the sixties, is now, in the late seventies, playing a major part as sponsor and manufacturer in the revival of the four-stroke machine.

In 1962, the bike he helped design and build with Husqvarna became the first two-stroke to win a World Championship, in his own hands. In 1977, the bike he helped design and build became the first four-stroke in seven years to win a Grand Prix, in the hands of Bengt Aberg.

Hallman's close involvement with development was always very much part of his success as a rider. An intelligent man, with an engineering degree from Gothenburg University, he was more than just a skilful scrambler. He was a perfectionist with a keen eye for preparation before, and tactics during a tough motocross race.

It was the professionalism in his outlook which made as much impact on the recent history of motocross as his determined racing and 37 Grands Prix wins. Hallman might never have gone into motocross at all. By the age of thirteen, he was already a promising junior football star in his native home of Skyttorp. But his elder brother, Hasse, was riding, and beating some of the top Swedish stars and, keen to emulate him, young 'Totte' took to borrowing his bike.

When he was sixteen, he began to ride competitively in trials on a 175cc Husqvarna and in the following year, 1959, notched up his first major success, and an international one at that. He took a Gold Medal at the Tatra Trial in Poland.

His riding caught the attention of the Husqvarna factory who loaned him a prototype 250cc machine to ride in motocross. A spell of compulsory military service intervened, however, and it was not until 1961 that he was able to compete his first full season of racing. When he did, he brought home the

Swedish 250cc Championship. From then on his career was meteoric.

In 1962 he swept into the World 250cc series and snatched what appeared to be an unassailable lead from Jeff Smith on BSA to take the title. He repeated the performance the following year, and though toppled by the Russian Victor Arbekov in 1964, came back again to win in 1966 and 1967, again on Husqvarna.

Hallman's World Championship record has been beaten only by Roger De Coster and Joel Robert, the man who finally stopped his runaway success. Both would have to admit, however, that it was Hallman who had an important influence on their early careers by his approach to the sport.

Further, on a tour sponsored by the Husqvarna factory, it was Hallman in the mid-sixties who did much to introduce motocross to America.

Hallman retired from serious Grand Prix competition in 1968. He tried to make a comeback in 1969, but an injured back, and finally a broken foot, decided him to bow out of the title chase. But he was still not about to quit motocross.

In 1971, after 15 years with Husqvarna, he was hired as development rider by Yamaha and did much of the early work on the factory's competition two-strokes, laying the foundations of an effort which in 1977 brought them their first motocross World Championship.

The relationship was further cemented as, in partnership, Hallman became the Swedish Yamaha importer, expanding a motor cycle business he had begun in Uppsala as early as 1968.

With another dealership in California, Hallman's motocross business, like his riding, became truly international. It was a combination of all these links that produced the prototype 500cc four-stroke Yamaha, and could yet carry the Hallman banner into a further decade of the sport.   MC

Below: Torsten Hallman in action on his Husqvarna during the 250cc British Grand Prix at Dodington in 1970. The following year saw him join Yamaha as a development rider

Walter Handley

*Below: Handley wins the 1933
Ulster GP on his Velocette*

FEW INDEED are the TT competitors 'honoured' (if
that's the right term) by having a corner on the Isle of
Man course named after them. There was Triumph
team leader Walter Brandish, who dropped his
Triumph just above Hillberry; Bill Doran, who came
off his AJS in the Glen Helen section; and a shy,
almost sulky Brummie called Wal Handley, who
cast away his Senior Rudge in 1932 and so gave a
name to the fast S-bend above Baarregarrow.

Wal was a complex character, a loner who
seemed to revel in adversity and was at his best when
the cards were stacked high against him. Like, for
instance, in the 1926 Senior TT, when his vee-twin
Rex-Acme had been giving trouble and Wal had had
to lose time at the pits. Roaring back into the race,
he bombed around to finish in an eventual runner-up
spot, a remarkable achievement.

Or, again, as in the Brooklands 200-miler of
the same year where he lost seventeen minutes on the
start line when a tyre went flat, and still finished
second, breaking a hatful of world speed records, up
to and including the 200 miles, in the process, an
achievement which few others could ever match.

A protege of OK Supreme boss, Ernie
Humphries, Wal Handley was thrown into the deep
end of road racing at only eighteen years of age – and
broke the lap record in his first event (the 1922 250cc
TT) from a standing start, only to retire on the next
lap. A few weeks later, in torrential rain, he was
second in the 250cc Belgian Grand Prix, after stopping
several times to dry out his magneto.

It was the Belgian, too, which gave him his
first classic win, a year later. From then on, there was
no stopping Wal. Joining the Rex-Acme team for 1925
(later, he became their competitions manager) he
pulled off the first ever double TT success in a single
week, a feat for which Birmingham gave him a civic

reception on his return.

More wins were to follow; for Rex-Acme, the 250cc TT again, in 1927; and for Rudge, the Senior (500cc) TT in 1930. There were other rides, too, on Husqvarnas, Velocettes, and Excelsiors, but not always with the best of fortune. After 1934, Wal switched to car racing, and he had been away from the motor cycle field for three years when he made an unexpected appearance at Brooklands in a mid-week BMCRC meeting with, of all things, a BSA.

What happened next is Brooklands history, because Wal rocketed around on the unfashionable Beesa, finishing at an average speed of 102.27mph,

and with one lap at 107.57mph. Now, it was the custom of the BMCRC organisers to award a gold lapel brooch in the shape of a star, to any rider beating 100mph in a race. So Wal won his Gold Star; and from the machine he rode that day, BSA evolved a new super-sports model named, from Wal's achievement, the Gold Star.

It is history, too, though of a less happy kind, that Wal Handley met his death in the autumn of 1941 when, as a captain in the Air Transport Auxiliary, the Airacobra fighter plane he was ferrying to an RAF base failed soon after taking off from a Cumberland airfield.   FG

Above: Handley (Excelsior) at the 1933 Lightweight TT

Below: Wal Handley (Rudge) pushes off at the start of the 1932 Senior TT unaware that his impending crash will put Handley's Cottage on the TT map

John Hartle

JOHN HARTLE's first major race meeting was at Oliver's Mount in 1954, and ironically it was at this same Scarborough circuit that the Norton, Gilera and MV Agusta works rider lost his life fourteen years later.

His debut on the Isle of Man, where he was to make a name for his consistent performances, came in 1955 when he finished a creditable sixth on his Junior Norton. In the Ulster GP later that season he showed more promise by finishing second to Lomas's Guzzis in both 350 and 500 races.

He was signed by Norton in 1956 to ride in what was to be the last season for the factory team. The TT was the first championship event that year and John started well with a third spot in the Junior and second in the Senior behind the MV Agusta of Surtees. Once again he did well in Ulster scoring his first Grand Prix victory in the 500cc race. With points from just two 500cc races, John finished third in the world championship.

After a second place in the 350 German GP on his private Norton, Hartle contested more of the Grands Prix in 1957 but could only finish the 350 championship in fifth place. At the request of Surtees he was given a ride on a 250 MV during the Belgian GP, which he won at a record speed.

Hartle was runner up to Surtees in both 350 and 500cc classes in 1958. In the smaller class he had finished second in five races. On the larger bike he had become the second rider to lap the Isle of Man at over the magic 100mph figure.

In 1959, Hartle was again runner up to Surtees in the Junior class, although an Italian team-mate had taken over the rides on the bigger machine. The next year John won his first TT, the Junior, and came second in the Senior. He also came second in the 350cc Ulster race, and won the 500 on a Norton, beating Surtees. After that Hartle was dropped by MV and finished the season on his own Nortons, coming third overall in both the larger classes.

He crashed heavily at Scarborough in 1961, and his injuries kept him out of racing for two years. When he returned in 1963 it was to ride the old Gileras which Geoff Duke had borrowed from the Italian factory. The season started well with second places in the Senior and Junior TTs, and then a win in the 500cc race at Assen, followed by another 2nd in Ulster. There was no catching Hailwood, however, and Hartle finished third overall in the championship.

Back on Nortons in 1964, John competed in the first US Grand Prix at Daytona finishing third, but later in the season he crashed heavily at Imola and was out of action for another two years.

When Hartle returned in 1967 it was with some satisfaction that he won the Hutchinson 100 and the first Isle of Man Production TT. In the world championship he was again third on a Matchless.

The following season he crashed twice on the Isle of Man, and later in the year while accelerating out of the hairpin at Scarborough he hit another rider and crashed receiving fatal injuries.   GE

Far right: Hartle at speed on the big 500cc MV at the Senior TT of 1968

Below: John Hartle on his 350 MV during the Isle of Man Junior TT of 1960

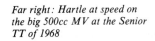

Gary Hocking

Right: Gary Hocking of Southern Rhodesia, World 350 and 500cc Champion in 1961. He rode for the Italian MV Agusta team

Below: Gary Hocking hustles his 350cc MV Agusta four through Tournagrough during the 1961 Ulster Grand Prix. He went on to win the Irish race in fine style

ALTHOUGH BORN in South Wales, Gary Hocking was brought up in Rhodesia, where, as a teenager, he started racing motor cycles on grass. After the usual succession of home built specials, he acquired a 350 Manx Norton on which he developed a taste for true road circuit racing.

Following in the steps of Ray Amm and Jim Redman, the young colonial came to Europe in his 21st year to join the 'Continental Circus'. In his first race, the 1958 500cc Dutch GP, he finished sixth; in the next round he was fourth and a few weeks later he came third behind the works MVs at the Nürburgring circuit in Germany.

Gary had immediately made his mark on the European scene and his world championship ambitions had been stimulated. At the first round of the 1959 season, in France, riding his Norton he split the works MVs in the 350 race and finished third in the highly competitive 500 class.

In his first TT he was twelfth on his 350 bike but at Hockenheim he once again came between the two MVs. Having been offered a ride on the East German works MZs, he won the 250 Swedish and Ulster Grands Prix, and at Belfast he also came second on a 125cc machine. That year he finished second in the 250 championship. He had scored several good results on his bigger Nortons, coming fifth in the 500 table and fourth in the 350 championship, but at the last Grand Prix in Italy, he finished sixth on a 125 MV and was awarded a place in the works team.

In 1960, with the full support of the MV factory behind him, Hocking really looked impressive. MV literally swept the board in every class and Gary was second in three of them, the 125cc, 250cc and 350cc. That year he won his first TT, the 250, but the championship he came closest to winning was that of the 350 class. Although Hocking had won two Grands Prix, the same number as John Surtees, the English rider had ensured his last title double by virtue of an extra third place.

After the 1960 season MV closed down its racing department, with the exception of some 350cc and 500cc fours, which Hocking and later Hailwood

were to ride under the MV-Privat label – a title which fooled no-one because the machines were proper works bikes in disguise.

After finishing second to Phil Read's Norton in the 350 TT, Gary went on to win four consecutive Grands Prix and the championship. In the 500cc class he won seven races, although hotly pursued by Hailwood who was MV mounted for the last three rounds. In achieving the championship double Gary was continuing the tradition which Surtees had begun for MV Agusta.

The 1962 season began on the Isle of Man. In the Junior TT Hocking finished second to his MV team mate but in that race his friend Tom Phillis had been killed and it affected Gary deeply. After he had gone out and won the Senior race he announced his retirement from motor cycle racing and returned to Rhodesia. In his brief career he had ridden straight to the top and shown himself to be a natural racing talent.

Later in the year, however, he was tempted back onto a race circuit by the lure of four wheeled Formula One racing. In December 1962 he was killed at the wheel of his car while practising for the Natal Grand Prix. It was a tragic irony that a young man who had won everything the world of two wheels had to offer should lose his life in a relatively unimportant motor car race. GE

Above: Hocking at speed on the 500cc MV at the Senior TT of 1962. After the race, he announced his retirement. Some time later he returned to the race track, this time as a car racer

Left: Hocking in action on the 'fire engine' MV Agusta 500

Bill Ivy

OF ALL THE road racers of the 'sixties era, Bill Ivy was perhaps the most dynamic and often the most controversial of the English contingent. 'Little Bill', the 5ft 3in tall rider from Maidstone, Kent, was happy on all classes of racing machinery but it was on the phenomenal 125cc Yamaha that he won his only world title.

Bill's racing career began at his local circuit of Brands Hatch, in 1959, where as a seventeen-year-old he first raced a 50cc Itom. Over the next few seasons, experience of short circuit racing was gained in all classes, on machines for various sponsors, and in 1964 Ivy won the 125cc ACU Star.

The following year, he won the star again on his Yamaha, took the 500 class honours on Tom Kirby's immaculate red and white Matchless G50 and won the British Championship, which at that time was decided by a single race. Contesting some of the Grands Prix for the first time, Bill finished fourth on his 125cc bike in two GPs, including the Japanese round where he also came third on a 250. Back home he was voted MCN Man of the Year and it came as no surprise when he was offered a big money contract to ride the multi-cylinder, lightweight Yamahas in 1966.

After winning three of the first four 125cc GPs, including the TT, Bill was in a good position to win the World Championship, but poor results for

Below: Bill Ivy in action on a Jawa 350 at Hockenheim in 1969. He was killed later that year in East Germany when the two-stroke, four-cylinder engine of the Jawa seized

With Hailwood out of 250 Grand Prix racing, Yamaha foresaw a clean sweep for themselves in both 125 and 250 classes during 1968. The two riders, Ivy and Read were under orders to share the titles, with Ivy scheduled to win the larger class. Bill obeyed and let Phil take the 125 title, but as soon as he was sure of that crown Read set about Ivy with a view to winning both championships. After an already exciting start to the season, things really hotted up towards the end and the Read–Ivy duel was continued in earnest – even on the home circuits. When Read squeezed the vital last race victory at Monza, both riders were equal on points and placings and the result of the championship was decided on race times, with Bill losing out by just two minutes.

Far right: Ivy on his way to winning the 1965 125cc TT on the works Yamaha

Ivy in the next few rounds helped Luigi Taveri take the title by six points. Ivy's last round win in Japan, however, was an important psychological boost for Yamaha, particularly as Bill also finished second to team-mate Phil Read in the 350cc race.

The following year was Bill's championship season and he made sure of the title this time with eight Grand Prix wins in the 125cc class, while on the 250 he was only four points behind the champion Hailwood, although in third place.

Dissillusioned with life on two wheels, Ivy retired from the sport and tried his luck with a Formula Two car in which he proved very impressive. He was soon enticed back to bikes, however, by an offer of a ride on the Jawa four-cylinder racers, for the Czechoslovakian factory. After a promising start for him, with two second places behind Ago's MV, the fifth round in East Germany brought disaster. While practising at Sachsenring, the Jawa seized and Bill was killed in the ensuing crash.　　GE

Arne Kring

Right: Kring hurls his Husqvarna round a corner during the 500cc British Motocross Grand Prix of 1975

Below: Arne Kring in action on his Husqvarna machine in 1969

Below right: a beaming Arne Kring pictured after the Swedish Grand Prix of 1969

Far right top: Kring airborne during the British Grand Prix of 1970. His machine is a Swedish-built Husqvarna

Far right bottom: Arne Kring (Husqvarna) leads the CZ of Mirec Kubicek during the 500cc Swiss Motocross Grand Prix of 1975. Kring, a Swede by birth, was one of the men responsible for the successful development of the Husqvarna machines during the late 1960s and early '70s

ARNE KRING now works in a little ski and sports supply shop next to his home in a little village near Alfta in Northern Sweden. It's a family business which he's been helping with for many years, and he's always enjoyed it. Life runs at an easy pace, especially in the long, cold winters.

When custom is slack, he goes out riding at the local track, or in the forests on a bike equipped with studded tyres to grip on the snow and ice. It was in conditions like that he learnt to control a motocross bike with superb skill. And though he doesn't race any more, Arne has not lost any of his talents.

He's just a little older, and a little wiser, and has learnt to accept that luck was never really on his side in motocross. For if it had been, there's no doubt that the records would have read Arne Kring, World Champion.

Arne's spell at the top of motocross competition was relatively short, but during that time he was one of the fastest and most spectacular men on two wheels. Injury was entirely the reason for his demise. Motocross riders are built to be resilient, but cracking his hip, two bones in his back, breaking a leg and dislocating a knee, all within a matter of months, proved too much for the wiry five-foot nine Swede.

Arne arrived on the scene late – at the age of 26. He had already been riding for ten years when he came, apparently from nowhere, to win the 500cc Swedish Grand Prix in 1969.

He'd started racing under the influence of his father-in-law who owned a cycle shop. With his support, Arne used to build his own frames around a 250cc Husqvarna engine. More often than not,

however, the homemade parts would break up underneath him.

Once, in 1963, they didn't, and Arne was second overall behind Torsten Hallman in the 250cc Swedish GP. 'But it was just sheer luck,' says Arne. 'It happened to be a sandy track which was my real favourite.' His promising ride was not followed up, and most people wrote it off as a flash in the pan.

It wasn't until late in 1968 in fact that Arne started to make any progress at all. What he had to learn was how to ride fast on all sorts of tracks, not just sand, and what he also discovered was that he was better on the larger five-hundred machines than the lightweight two-fifties.

At the start of the 1969 season, he scraped together all his savings and bought a 400cc Husqvarna. On it he shot to immediate success, winning both races of the Swedish GP, and going on to be overall winner of the following round in Holland. His victories brought him the backing of the Husqvarna factory, but not the title which that year went instead to team mate Bengt Aberg.

Everyone expected 1970 would be his season, however. He led the whole way till July, when with three rounds to go he only had to finish fourth in one race to clinch the World Championship on aggregate points total. While racing at a national meeting at Ostend, however, he crashed heavily, his bike landing on top of him and cracking his pelvis, two vertebrae, and causing severe bruising.

He was back on his feet again within an incredible three weeks, but doctors refused to allow him to race and the title went again to Aberg. Arne didn't ride again until much later in the year, but then, in America, he broke his leg. Early in 1971, he dislocated his knee.

The injuries came too quickly upon each other and were compounded by the disappointment of coming so near and yet so far from the title. Still backed by Husqvarna, he continued to race the GPs for another five years, always capable of finishing among the top handful, but was never again a threat to the title. Arne retired officially from international competition at the end of 1976.   MC

Sten Lundin

THEY CALLED Sten Lundin 'the Stork', not just because he was a tall, lanky man, well over six foot, but because of the way he craned his body over a motocross bike when racing. The style was not so much an affectation as a necessity. For the bikes Sten raced weighed over 300lb and had barely three inches of suspension movement. Instead of soaking up the bumps, they bulldozed them, or bounced off, and you had to be a big man, and an alert one, to hang on.

Sten's stature meant he could hang on better than most, and he used it to full effect. He won his first world championship at the age of 29, in 1959; was runner up to fellow Swede Bill Nilsson in 1960; and won it back in 1961. In addition he was placed third in the 500cc world championship class six times in his career at the top.

Sten started racing in the early '50s, when continental motocross was still young, and Sweden was virtually unknown as a source for talent. Along with Nilsson, he was one of the first to make the other Europeans sit up and take notice of Scandinavia.

His first bikes were basically British – much modified BSA twin-cylinder models – but the real breakthrough came when Sweden began to produce her own. Factories like Husqvarna and Monark were long established but only with the rise of top Swedish riders did they begin to take a serious interest in motocross.

Both companies used 500cc overhead valve single-cylinder motors developed from military usage. They still had BSA gearboxes and clutches, however, while the forks were Norton. On a Monark with those specifications, Sten won the 1959 World Championship, only the second Swede to snatch the coveted title from Britain and Belgium.

For 1961 he switched to another Swedish mount, the Lito, which had a similar engine but a shorter stroke, making it rev higher and produce more power at speed. It was on the big 270lb Lito that Lundin had most of his success, both in the World Championship, and in many international meetings over the following eight years.

The writing was on the wall, however, for the overweight and obsolete engines. Already two-strokes had made rapid inroads into the 250cc class and were beginning to make their presence felt among the 500s.

Along with this trend came lighter four-stroke engines, basically over-bored two-fifties, like the BSA on which Jeff Smith was to take the title in 1964 and 1965. The bikes were easier to control than the monsters that only men like 'the Stork' could handle.

Lundin tried hard to block this trend, and campaigned for the big class to be opened out with engines up to 750cc. He was convinced that the sight of big men wrestling with big bikes was the only worthwhile spectacle in motocross.

He was running against the tide though. The FIM bowed and introduced a 750cc international class in 1966, but it was only over a handful of rounds, and was supported indifferently. It never had the appeal of the World Championship proper, and was condemned to be an also-ran series. Sten won it, nevertheless, using his familiar Lito bored-out to 508cc. In 1967, as well as being 750cc champion, he notched up twenty major international victories.

Such performances showed that, even at the age of 37, he was still among the top riders in the world, but he couldn't adapt to the changes that were altering the face of the Grands Prix. At the same time he was developing a successful alternative career as a rally driver competing internationally.

Sten officially retired from racing motocross in 1969. Even then he went out on what was basically a ten-year-old Lito, but under the Monark factory banner, and was beating up-to-date 400cc Husqvarna two-strokes in Swedish national events.

He was never quite able to stay away from bikes though. At the end of 1976 he designed the frame for Bengt Aberg's 500cc Yamaha Grand Prix machine, and was tempted out on a similar mount to ride in the Swedish four-stroke championship the following year. At 47, the oldest competitor, he was still among the most stylish. However, his stubborn resolution to campaign a distinctly outmoded and technologically unevolved machine resulted in an inability to prove competitive against the new generation of two-stroke powered bikes, forcing him to take a back seat in World Championships. MC

Bottom: Sten Lundin in action at Farleigh Castle on his Lito in 1966

Below: Lundin at Hawkstone Park in 1974

Far left: Lundin powers his Monark round Hawkstone Park in 1960. The Monark was a Swedish built machine using an ohv single-cylinder motor. In 1959 Lundin used a Monark to win the 500cc World Motocross Championship

Bob McIntyre

Far right: 'Bob Mac' at speed on his 500 Norton during the 1956 Hutchinson 100 at Silverstone

Glasgow in 1928, he took to road racing after scrambling, and made his debut in an amateur event on a borrowed 350cc BSA Gold Star. His first visit to the Isle of Man in 1952 brought him second place in the Senior Manx Grand Prix, on a Junior machine! He later displayed magnificent talent with a second place in the Junior TT of 1955, a remarkable lap in excess of 99mph in the 1958 Senior TT and those momentous battles against works MVs in the 1959 Junior and Senior TTs – all on production Norton and AJS racing machines.

Early in his career, McIntyre formed an enduring and highly successful partnership with ace-tuner, entrant and sponsor, Joe Potts, riding Nortons and AJSs. This partnership was changed reluctantly by both men after British machinery had become so uncompetitive that only by accepting offers from Gilera and, later, Honda, did both men agree that McIntyre would have any chance of achieving his ambition of a world title; although, even then, Bob continued to ride Joe Potts'-tuned machinery whenever possible.

McIntyre was equally at home on short and long circuits and, although his career spanned a decade, he was a works rider for only three seasons: AJS in 1954, Gilera (as team leader) in 1957 and Honda in 1962. He came nearest to a world title in 1957 when he ended the season in second place in both the 350cc and 500cc classes. Adding to his impressive victory on the Isle of Man with second places at Hockenheim and Ulster, McIntyre only needed to win the final grand prix of the season at Monza to take the 500cc world title. However, he was unwell and could not complete in the event.

Shortly after the withdrawal of Gilera from racing at the end of 1957, McIntyre took a 350cc

BOB MCINTYRE will always be remembered as the first rider to lap the Isle of Man at over 100mph, and his historic ride on a red and white Gilera four in the second lap of the Senior TT, on 7 June 1957, pushed the record to 101.03mph. On the fourth lap, he did even better at 101.12mph, and altogether rode with such command that four laps of the 8-lap race were taken in excess of 100mph for a momentous victory at a race average of 98.99mph.

'Bob Mac', as he was affectionately known, was a dedicated and highly respected rider. Born in

Below: McIntyre setting a record lap of 99.58mph during the 1961 Lightweight TT. Four years earlier, McIntyre became the first man to lap the Isle of Man at over 100mph

Gilera four to Monza and shattered the world one hour record at a dazzling 141mph, a record which stood until 1964 when Mike Hailwood was fractionally faster at Daytona.

The loan of a Honda in 1961 led to a contract with the Japanese factory for 125cc and 250cc classic events in 1962. A significant win in Belgium and second places in Spain, France, Holland and Germany, left him usefully placed for the 250cc world title, but the season ended prematurely in disaster. At 33 years of age and at the peak of his career, Bob McIntyre crashed a five-speed experimental Norton at Oulton Park in August and eventually died from his injuries.   PC

Below: Bob McIntyre in action on a 500cc Gilera (right) and a Bianchi twin (left)

Jack Milne

THE TALL, tungsten-muscled Jack Milne was born in Buffalo, New York in 1910, where his father, a Scotsman, was in business. At the age of fifteen he moved with his family to Detroit and completed his education at Pasadena High School.

The young American developed an intense interest in anything mechanical and on leaving school he secured a position at the famous Ford Motor works. Here, in the midst of automobile engines, he soon became a proficient engineer. In the meantime, Jack's younger brother Cordy had taken up speedway racing. The two brothers had each owned ordinary road machines but Cordy had converted his into what he considered to be a good track model. It wasn't, but he had at least started on the trail which was to lead both of them on a tour of American, Australian and British speedways.

As 1933 came round, two Comerford-JAPs from England arrived for the brothers. This made for faster racing, keener competition, and tougher battles on the track. Just previously Jack had recovered from his first serious crash, which occurred at San Diego. At this time he was also racing at circuits such as San Francisco, Santa Ana, Long Beach and several others in the Los Angeles area. To stand near the first bend at any of these renowned tracks was to experience an adrenalin rush more intense than that caused by almost anything else. The air was split with the incredible roar of powerful bikes at full song and the ground shook as if the tremors were of a small but devastating earthquake.

On the new JAP machines Jack and Cordy began to win a host of events, giving many mesmerising performances. Unfortunately, in 1934 Jack sustained an injury which kept him out of the American National Championship. He and Putt Mossman were involved in a crash which left Jack in hospital with a crushed vertebra – it was an accident which very nearly ended his career.

Far right: Jack Milne poses on his JAP-engined speedway machine in 1937. That was a particularly successful year for the American because he not only won the Australian championship, but the World Championship as well. This made him the first – and still the only – American ever to have taken the world speedway crown

Below: Jack Milne, seated on the Excelsior, shakes hands with Bill Kitchen, another leading speedway rider of the early 1930s

Although it took many months, Jack eventually made a miraculous recovery and, on returning to racing, he became runner-up to Cordy in the American National Championship.

At the end of the season Jack and Cordy went to Australia, where they thought the third-of-a-mile Sydney track the best in the world, faster and easier to ride than any in the USA. The trip was highly successful in other ways too. 'The Australian hospitality was unbelievable,' remarked Jack in an interview, and to complete his delight he won the Australian Championship too.

The two brothers then moved on to England. Both wished to ride for New Cross, but the ACU refused permission. Jack could go to New Cross but Cordy was allocated to Hackney.

Just as the two Americans were getting used to British circuits, Jack was involved in an accident at West Ham in which he lost his left thumb when he took evasive action to avoid a fallen rider. Toughman Jack was soon in the saddle again, however, and riding as well as ever. He became one of the top stars of the New Cross Team, winning the Farndon Memorial Trophy and gaining tenth place in the World Championship.

Then came 1937. In that season Jack was really at the top. He won the Australian Championship once again and beat the sport's best in gaining the London Riders' Championship at Wembley. With his chest emblazoned with the Stars and Stripes and with several amazing rides, he reached the pinnacle of his career by winning the World Championship – the first, and still the only, American to accomplish the feat. Jack's fellow countryman Wilbur Lamoreaux came second and brother Cordy was third.

Jack almost repeated his dazzling Championship performance in 1938, but was narrowly edged out by Bluey Wilkinson.

The National League was won by New Cross, primarily on account of Jack's tremendous riding. In the following season, with enviable energy and enthusiasm, he won the London Riders' Championship again, but as World War II started in late 1939 the two illustrious brothers returned to America, notching up a host of further successes until their country joined the conflict after 1941.

When speedway resumed in 1946 the renowned Milne brothers were among the first to begin racing again. Jack was as good as ever, taking second spot in the American Championship. In the same event two years later he gained the same placing this time as runner-up to brother Cordy. The following year however, saw a decline in American speedway and Jack rode only at Los Angeles in 1950. A few years later, speedway died in the States which brought about the racing retirement of Jack Milne . . . one of the world's greatest riders. CM

Derek Minter

*Opposite page, clockwise:
Minter leading Alan Shepherd
at Mallory Park in 1963 during
a 350cc race and on his Norton
(29) at Brands Hatch in 1960;
at Blandfor in 1959 on another
Norton (55); aboard a 350cc
production Ducati at Brands in
1968; and urging the unusual
Cotton Norton round Brands*

DEREK MINTER was an immaculate, outstanding rider and a great character. Outspoken, independent and sometimes too critical of humbug and authority for his own good, he was undoubtedly the best short circuit rider of his day.

His record in 1962 was outstanding, even for Minter. He was at his peak then, winning repeatedly at all the major British circuits. At Brands Hatch, where he was the local hero and for many years their uncrowned King, he rode in five races in one day, won five times and created five records. He became British Champion that year, for the third time, won Mallory Park's 1000 guineas race, the richest in Britain; and was voted *Man of the Year* in a national poll.

It was also in 1962, in the Isle of Man, that he created a sensation by winning the 250cc TT on a year-old non-works Honda, against the power – and to the embarrassment – of the official works team.

Derek Minter was born the son of a pit worker in Kent. His first bike was a 350cc BSA, bought from what could be saved from his £1 a week earnings as an electrician's mate with the Canterbury bus company and a supplementary £2 he made from spare-time apple picking. That was in 1948. Ten years later, after local sponsorships, he turned full-time professional. As he left that year to prove himself on the Isle of Man the only money he possessed was £100 in his Post Office savings account. He finished fourth in the Senior and ninth in the Junior races. In 1960 he entered nine Easter programme races and won eight of them. Later that year he became the first man to lap the TT course on a single-cylinder machine at a speed over 100mph.

On the mainland circuits like Brands Hatch, Mallory, Oulton Park, Snetterton and Castle Combe, Minter quickly became supreme. His form at Brands Hatch was devastating and he was the automatic choice as the circuit's uncrowned King after former hero John Surtees had forsaken bikes to turn his attention to racing cars.

Minter found it hard to submit to the discipline of being a team member. His works rides were consequently sporadic and the short time he spent in possession of a factory contract was an injustice to

*Below: demonstrating his neat
and tidy riding style at
Scarborough in 1963 on the
Scuderia Geoff Duke Gilera 500
four. Minter was a master of all
machines on a variety of circuits
all over Britain. His career was
centred around the local short
circuits and his forays into
international European racing
were limited*

his talent and craft as a rider. Traditionally a poor starter, he loved to weave his way through the pack, often storming through to win on the final lap, to delight and thrill his fans.

A great thing about Derek Minter was his mastery of machines, from the big Norton on which he made his name, and the Italian Gilera, to EMC, AJS, REG, MV, Benelli, Honda, Matchless and numerous others. He rode them all with consummate ease and never did he look out of his element.

'The Mint', as he was affectionately known, was the first rider to crack the 90mph barrier at Brands Hatch and he set countless records on British circuits, some of which he held for many years. In an outstanding career he had two major disappointments: not being offered a works contract by Honda after his winning of the 1962 TT on one of their

machines; and Gilera's refusal to return to racing in the 1960s, for his infrequent outings on the famous Italian machine, including an unofficial lap record at Monza at 120.75mph, showed his obvious potential as a fully international rider.

His breezy manner, forthrightness, immaculate style and professionalism, made Derek Minter a man to admire and respect. He rode his final race in 1967 to end an era . . .and to start his own haulage business.

It is extremely unfortunate that this great rider did not get the necessary backing from the factories, as his unquestionable ability would have provided race-goers with even more spectacular wins. However it seems that his headstrong attitude outweighed his merits as a rider in the estimation of the selectors, and he retired.   PC

Bill Nilsson

BILL NILSSON, the Swedish motocross star of the late fifties and early sixties, is remembered primarily for two things. One is that he was the first motocross 'world' champion in 1957, the year the 500cc title was upgraded from 'European'. Secondly, and perhaps more memorably, he fired the imagination of the fans throughout Europe with his unusual machine. It was basically an AJS, although there was nothing basic about this mount. The engine was a much-modified 7R, the British company's well known road-racing unit, while the gearbox was BSA.

This machine became almost as famous as its rider. Originally owned by Olle Nygren, who won the 1955 Swedish National Championship on it, Nilsson bought it partly on the recommendation of Harold Taylor to whom Bill was something of a protégé. During the winter of 1956/57 the machine was re-built in the Stockholm workshops of Hans Osterman by the former TT rider Hildor Jansson. The bore was increased, the stroke lengthened, the head modified and the compression ratio was raised to 9.6 to 1.

Nilsson himself carried out modifications such as fitting a new kick-start equipped gearbox, a re-shaped petrol tank, 19 inch and 21 inch rims on the original road-racing conical hubs, longer forks and reshaping the top frame tube. The result was a very

Above right: Nilsson in action on his ESO at Hawkstone Park in 1965

Below: Nilsson on the 500cc Crescent at Hawkstone Park in 1958

potent war-horse which struck a resounding chord with nearly everyone in the sport, not least of all his respectful opponents.

Those opponents, like Bill, are now bastions of motocross history, Sten Lundin, Rene Baeten, Auguste Mingels, Les Archer, Geoff Ward, Jeff Smith and John Draper. It was in such company that the likeable Swede found fame and glory. As Sweden developed as a scrambling nation, her riders improved to become a real force in continental meetings. In 1954, Nilsson took a BSA to Assen in Holland for the annual Moto Cross des Nations and won. As Britain's Les Archer said: 'Bill Nilsson had proved himself to be Sweden's number one rider'.

This yearly international battle became a happy hunting ground for Bill. In 1955, again on a home-tuned BSA, he led his country's team to victory. In 1958, the event was held at Kagerod in southern Sweden where he thrilled the home crowd with a fine show of supremacy; he was now riding the famous AJS. In 1961, back in Holland, Nilsson, riding a four-stroke Husqvarna left everyone behind as he led from start to finish.

However, his finest year must be 1957 when he won not only his first but *the* first 500cc Motocross World Championship. On the 7R AJS he won the Swedish and Italian Grands Prix, came second in the French and went on later to take third place in the Danish and Belgian rounds. At the height of the summer he came to Hawkstone Park for the British Grand Prix where, in spite of fierce opposition, he took fifth place. At the end of the season the undisputed king of motocross was Bill Nilsson.

The Swede fought a bitter duel in 1958 with the Belgian Rene Baeten and finally had to accept a narrow defeat. In 1960, however, he came back with a Husqvarna and once more the world crown was his.

Nilsson continued to ride in international motocross events well into the sixties but in 1965, after more than a decade in top flight competition, he had an off-track head-on collision with Rolf Tibblin while both men were machine testing. Nilsson suffered a broken arm and later faded from the motocross scene entirely. It was a sad ending for a star who ranked among the greatest. RB

Above left: Bill Nilsson's AJS at Brands Hatch in 1957

Below: in action on the big Husqvarna, also at Hawkstone Park, in 1960

Eric Oliver

MALLORY PARK has rarely seen a sidecar battle as fierce as that which enlivened the Vintage Race of the Year meeting in May of 1978. With his one-time crewman Stan Dibben back on the passenger platform, Eric Oliver was using every ounce of trackcraft to edge his Norton outfit past the flying 650cc Triumph of Roger Allen; and the crowd were loving it because, shrugging off his 67 years, Eric was demonstrating in full measure just why he had been World Champion back in 1949 (the first year that the sidecar championship was run) and for several years thereafter.

Yet even that had been a second career for Eric Oliver. Born in Crowborough, Sussex, he began his competitive career in 1931 as a solo grass-tracker, hitting the heights in southern meetings some three years later on a self-tuned 1924 big port AJS.

In due course there came a speedway JAP-engined Rudge, but by then Eric was riding on the hard stuff also, using a camshaft Velocette and an Excelsior-JAP at short circuits such as the newly opened Cadwell Park. He tried the TT, too, tackling the 1937 Senior with a Vincent-HRD, only to drop out with a broken oil pipe, and not until 1939 did he score a finish – this time with a Mk VIII KTT Velocette. Using the same bike, he claimed fifteenth places in both the Junior and Senior events.

Eric began sidecar racing, on the grass, in 1936, but this was something of a sideline, and not until after World War II (in which he was an RAF Flight-Lieutenant, carrying out bombing missions over Europe) did he gradually switch the emphasis from solo to sidecar work.

Remember the passengers of those early road-racing days? Les Nutt, and 'Jenks' (Denis Jenkinson), the bearded wonder, Lorenzo Dobelli, Stan Dibben and Eric Bliss.

When Eric began, road-racing sidecars were still bolt-on adjuncts to a relatively standard solo motor cycle, and in many instances were totally unstreamlined adaptations of grass-track chairs, with welded-on handholds in profusion, to assist the passenger in his necessary acrobatics.

True, Eric was not the first to switch to a clear platform with streamlined nose and sidecar mudguard (that honour should go to Arthur Horton), but he certainly stood the sidecar racing world on its collective ear by introducing the first-ever fully-faired kneeler. Designed by *Motor Cycle* artist Laurie Watts, it broke new ground in various directions, notably in that it was a machine conceived as a whole; the familiar motor cycle frame was discarded and, instead, the Manx Norton engine was installed in an integral space-frame, with ducts built into the light-alloy bodywork to deliver cooling air to the engine.

The importance of this outfit cannot be stressed too highly, because its success was such that

Above right: Eric Oliver, the British ace who won the world sidecar championship in 1949, '50, '51 and 1953

Right: Eric Oliver's Norton at the German Grand Prix of 1955

other drivers had to evolve streamlined kneelers if they were to stay in the hunt. In subsequent seasons the Oliver streamliner was progressively developed, in the course of which programme it introduced the 10-in-diameter sidecar wheel.

Eric Oliver retired from active sport in 1955, but he had one more surprise for the racing public up his sleeve. In 1958, he made a comeback in the Sidecar TT – not with a racing outfit, but with a road-going Norton Dominator 88 twin, coupled to a touring Watsonian Monaco sidecar in which Mrs Pat Wise remained normally seated. It was more a bit of fun than a serious attempt to win, but for all that Eric finished in tenth position (with a bronze replica to show for it) at just under 60mph average speed; compare that with the 74.07mph record lap put in by winner Walter Schneider (BMW), and you'll have to agree that, for a swan song, it hit a pretty high note! FG

Above: Eric Oliver seen here at a grass-track racing event held at Brands Hatch in 1946

Below: Oliver is seen here with the KTT Velocette he rode to fifteenth place in both the Isle of Man Junior and Senior TT events of 1939

Jack Parker

Above right: a very fast family – Jack Parker (left) poses with his brother Norman

Below: Jack Parker pictured in action during speedway's fiftieth anniversary celebration meeting at Hackney in 1978. In the lower picture, he is seen leading current ace Malcolm Simmons, captain of England

THERE WERE many fabulous reputations built on the speedways in its golden age between 1927 and 1940, but none stands higher in retrospect than that of Jack Parker. Many of his distinguished contemporaries in speedway have characterised him as 'the greatest Englishman of them all'. And the list includes the late Frank Arthur, that illustrious Australian rider, who probably saw more of Jack during the late 'twenties and through the 'thirties than anyone else.

Jack's admirers were not confined to the ranks of speedway enthusiasts for, before climbing the speedway ladder, he had already carved out a name for himself in the motor cycle competition world as a brilliant trials rider.

Joining the BSA company's experimental department, he tuned the works trials machines for the classic national trials and, as a 20-year-old, took his place along with the other 238 competitors in the 1927 Colmore Cup Trial held over a 121-mile course which proved exceptionally severe, eventually causing 32 retirements.

Jack was driving a BSA combination with

brother Norman in the sidecar, and they won a silver medal in one of the toughest of all Colmores Trials. The following year he won the event outright.

Speedway, or Dirt-Track Racing as it was then known, was now being established in Britain; meanwhile Jack continued his winning ways in reliability trials and long-distance events in the official BSA team with John Humphries and Bert Perrigo.

On Whit-Saturday 1928 Jack made his first-ever appearance in Dirt-Track. This was at the King's Oak circuit, uniquely situated in the heart of Epping Forest. Stripping his BSA roadster of its sidecar, one footrest, a headlamp and other odds and ends, and replacing the four-gallon petrol tank with a small container, he was given sixteen seconds start in the Handicap race, the scratch man being Roger Frogley. By the end of the afternoon, however, Jack was a scratch man as well!

He was offered £15 and a match race with Vic Huxley to ride in the evening at Wimbledon in International Speedway's opening meeting by its chief, A. J. Hunting, and although outclassed and amazed by Huxley's magnificent riding, Jack received £75 for his efforts in the two meetings at the end of the day. It was good money . . . and he yearned for more!

The BSA Dirt-Track model that Jack Parker first built became, with one or two modifications, the BSA works machine which sold at £65. His company then built at the rear of its Birmingham factory, a dirt-track circuit costing £2000 for Jack's exclusive use in individually testing every model produced.

Jack rose to speedway stardom very quickly indeed and when league racing began in 1929, he captained the Coventry team. From then on, throughout his career, he remained a skipper; Southampton, Clapton, Lea Bridge, Harringey and Belle Vue were his teams. From the renowned Vic Huxley, he gained the World Championship in '31, after one of the most titanic struggles the speedway game had ever seen.

Representing his country in a host of England versus Australia test matches over a considerable period, Jack also captained the national team on many occasions, and at 47, when he retired from the sport after 27 years of racing, he still remained as supreme top-scorer for those illustrious matches with no less than 460 points!

Continuing his winning ways in his usual exuberant style, Jack won the Star Championship in '34 and gained fourth place in the World Championship of '37. He remained the peerless track tactician until World War II stopped all national racing. It resumed in '46 and 'Jolly Jack' was back again, but this time in Belle Vue colours. He topped the League score chart with 217 points, and having once got a grip on the Golden Helmet Match Race Championship title from Bill Kitchen, he never let go and, over a five-year period (1946–51), defeated no less than twenty-four challengers – an incredible individual speedway record.

Jack took third place in the '46 British Riders' Championship, led England to victory in two of the three test matches against Australia and took his team to their second post-war triumph in the National Trophy contests.

Another of the greatest of his many triumphs came the following season when he won the British Riders' Championship. Two years later – in the FIM World Championship – he gained second spot to Tommy Price.

A further Australian season of racing came for the 42-year-old rider in 1950–51 and Jack was undefeated in the Test series, won the New South Wales Championship and the valuable Jubilee

Championship Trophy.

So 'JP', the pipe smoker and Chairman of the Speedway Riders' Association for many years, gallantly kept on racing. But 'Anno Domini' was slowly telling a tale and in 1953 the wily old campaigner made that season his 'final fling'. CM

Above: Jack Parker (seated) with the England speedway team in 1948

Below: Parker in action at the Speedway in Melbourne

Tom Phillis

Opposite page, clockwise from top: Tom Phillis with wife and baby daughter; on the 250cc Honda four during the 1960 Ulster GP; practising at the Isle of Man during 1960; and on the Honda 250 (26) during the 1961 French Grand Prix

FROM AUSTRALIA have come many exciting riders to gain fame and fortune on the motor cycle race circuits of the world. Tom Phillis was one. He had the vision to recognise the potential of Honda as early as 1959, when most people were looking at the Japanese factory's early European efforts with subdued amusement. He became their team leader and brought them one of their two World Championships in 1961.

Tom Phillis started racing in Australia where a succession of falls brought him the nickname of 'autumn leaves'. By 1958 he was in Europe, but his debut on the Isle of Man that year was hardly devastating: 18th in the Senior and 32nd in the Junior, riding a Norton. Not until he signed for Honda did he make an impact. That was in March 1960. His first races for Honda were on the Isle of Man that year, when he finished 10th in the 125cc class and retired in the 250cc race. Shortly afterwards he crashed while in practice for the Dutch TT and this led to Jim Redman getting his chance with Honda. By this time Honda were making enough significant noises for a procession of riders to want to join them, but Tom

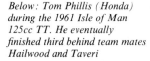

Below: Tom Phillis (Honda) during the 1961 Isle of Man 125cc TT. He eventually finished third behind team mates Hailwood and Taveri

Phillis and Jim Redman were good friends and once Phillis had recommended Redman to the Honda officials, they were happy to give the talented Rhodesian his chance. Thus is was through Phillis that the long and distinguished association between Redman and Honda was started.

In 1961 Honda were determined to succeed and flooded the classics with works machines. Phillis rode as team leader with Redman and Luigi Taveri, signed from MV, while machines were put out on loan to Bob McIntyre and a promising newcomer called Mike Hailwood. Tom started the season in devastating form, winning the 125cc race in Spain and finishing second to Gary Hocking on the MV in the 250cc event. Thereafter, Phillis and Ernst Degner, on the basically faster East German MZ machine, embarked on a season-long battle for the 125cc crown. Degner won in Germany, Phillis in France and Holland, Degner again in East Germany.

While in Sweden Degner had abandoned his machine and defected to the West in one of racing's most dramatic incidents. He held a slender lead over Tom Phillis as they travelled to the Argentine for the final grand prix of the season. Although Degner prepared to do battle on a borrowed EMC, the East Germans suspended his competition licence. Redman became Phillis' major threat, but the Australian crossed the line a fraction of a second ahead of Redman to take the 125cc world title. Victory in the 250cc race gave him second place in the highly contested 250cc world championship.

Likeable, easy-going, even slow-moving out of the saddle, Tom Phillis was transformed when he mounted a racing bike. Not a reckless rider, he was certainly extremely fast and rose instinctively to a challenge. It was perhaps this which contributed to his untimely death the very next year. Honda decided to have a go at winning the Junior TT on a 250 machine bored out to 285cc. The Italian MVs ridden by Hailwood and Gary Hocking were faster machines, but Phillis persuaded Redman, who should have ridden the bike, to let him take up the challenge. He kept the Honda in touch with Hocking and Hailwood in spite of its difficult handling. He desperately wanted to beat the MVs, which had won the race for the previous four years, and was moving very quickly into corners and obviously racing close to the limits. On the second lap, at Laurel Bank, he hit the wall and was killed.   PC

Ray Pickrell

Right: Pickrell on the works BSA 750 at Mallory Park

Far right top: Pickrell (8) dices with John Cooper (7) and Phil Read at Brands in 1972

Far right centre: Pickrell (Norton, 7) passes Griff Jenkins at Brands in 1966

Far right bottom: Pickrell on the Dunstall 750 in 1969

Below: Ray Pickrell (650 Triumph Bonneville) at the Brands 500-miler in 1965

LONDON RIDER Ray Pickrell was born in 1938 and began his road racing career in the early 1960s on the almost obligatory single-cylinder Manx Nortons. It was with the next generation of British bikes, the 650 and 750 twins and triples, that he shot to supremacy on the British circuits. He went on to win four 750 class TTs and countless short circuit races, but only occasionally raced on the continent and he did not contest the grands prix, despite his obvious competency in this field.

After campaigning his own machines for the first few seasons, Ray rode bikes supplied by tuner Geoff Monty, and his performances on short circuits earned him second spot in the 1965 Grovewood Awards. At a time when the twin-cylinder Norton Dominator looked like a successor to the legendary Manx, at least in the absence of real race machinery.

Pickrell was chosen to ride for Paul Dunstall.

South London tuner Dunstall had acquired the Norton race department and his Domiracers were blowing off the singles in the 1000cc races which had recently been introduced. In 1968, the Pickrell/Dunstall combination proved virtually unbeatable: Ray won the 750cc class of the Production TT, on his first visit, with a lap just under the magic 'ton'; at Brands Hatch, his home circuit, he won the big bike races at no less than six meetings, including the production event at the Hutchinson 100. The following season was only slightly less successful for Ray and he stayed with Dunstall until 1970, during which season he finished third in the Production TT.

In 1971, with the return of the British factory race teams, Pickrell was signed to ride the works BSA threes, on which he had an outstanding season: he was joint top scorer in the Anglo American Match Race series, after winning three of the six races; he

finished first with Percy Tait in the Bol d'Or 24hr endurance race at Le Mans; he came first in the Thruxton 500 miler; at the TT he won the 750cc Production race on *Slippery Sam* and came second in the Formula 750 race, setting a fastest lap of 105.68 mph; at Mallory Park Pickrell finished third in the Race of the Year, behind Cooper and Agostini; and finished the season in second place in the Superbike series, just six points behind Percy Tait.

Riding Triumphs in 1972 Ray was again top British scorer in the Match races, and endeared himself to the home fans by being the only man to beat Cal Rayborn and his Harley-Davidson. As well as winning on many of the short circuits that season, he pulled off a TT double, taking both the F750 and 750cc Production races. Later in the year he crashed heavily at Mallory Park, sustaining injuries which were serious enough to curtail his racing career. In what proved to be his last season Pickrell had once again finished second in the Superbike Championship but, perhaps more importantly, he had been voted Man of the Year by British enthusiasts.   GE

Tommy Robb

Right: Tommy Robb at the 1962 Lightweight TT riding the works Honda

Below: Tommy Robb piloting a production Suzuki 250 in a 500 mile endurance race in 1966

TOMMY ROBB, Northern Ireland's most successful road racer, was born in 1935 and won his first race on the dirt at sixteen years of age. He went road racing, which in Ulster means racing on *real* roads, when he was twenty and was soon winning races on a 175 MV. He later rode various machines including AJS Matchless, Norton, Ducati and NSU, for different sponsors and teams.

The next year Robb was signed by English tuner Geoff Monty to ride the latter's 250 GMS. Robb improved on his TT performance with an exciting fourth place behind the works MVs, and followed up with another fourth at the Ulster Grand Prix. At the end of the season he rode an MZ into sixth place in the 250 Italian Grand Prix.

In 1960, he was riding for Bultaco, but an accident on the Isle of Man put him out for much of the season. Back on the four-stroke singles for the 1961 season, Robb became Irish 500cc Champion. An outing to the Swedish Grand Prix late in the season brought him a third place on his AJS.

Tommy's biggest year came in 1962 when he was signed up by the Honda team and raced in four classes. He began with points-scoring rides in the 50cc races, but his performances on the 125 bikes were even more consistent, with several second and third places, including a second to Luigi Taveri in the TT. In the 250 class, however, Robb had his first grand prix win; fittingly enough it was at the Ulster Grand Prix meeting, at which he also finished second on a 125 and third on a 350. In the last 350 Grand Prix of the season Tommy beat Jim Redman, to win the race and take third spot in the World Championship, a position he equalled in the 125 class.

Still with Honda in 1963 Tommy did not win a grand prix, although his consistency earned him fourth place in the 250 World Championship. In 1964 he won many short circuit races on the 125 and 250 Hondas but did not figure in the classics. Given a try out by Yamaha, Robb finished third in the Dutch and fourth in the Belgian Grands Prix, but for his next

Left: Tommy Robb one of Ireland's most successful road racers

Below: Robb racing a Seeley (2) during 1971

factory ride the Ulsterman returned to Bultaco. His best placing on the Spanish bike in the 1965 classics was sixth in the Ulster 125 race, although the bikes were more competitive in the British national races. In 1966 the Bultacos fared a little better and Tommy had one of his best results at the Ulster GP with a third place in the 350 race behind Hailwood and Ago.

Tommy's form in grands prix continued over the following seasons with placings in several classes on Yamahas, Aermacchis and Seeleys, as well as on Bultacos. In 1970, riding a big four-stroke once again, Robb finished fourth in the 500cc World Championship standings.

In 1973, after almost twenty years of road racing and with 29 TT replicas to his credit, the 38-year-old rider won his first TT, the 125 race. He retired at the end of the year but maintained his links with the sport as the regular TT race commentator at Ballacraine.   GE

Cecil Sandford

CECIL SANDFORD was a British rider who first rode a competition motor cycle on grass in the late 1940s. Soon after, he graduated to the tarmac tracks and went on to ride a variety of works bikes in a brief but successful career.

Sandford's first season of serious grand prix competition was in 1950, when he campaigned a 350cc AJS on which he finished fifth in the Ulster Grand Prix, and sixth at the Italian round. His talent had already been noticed by the factory teams and, in 1951, Cecil rode works Velocettes, in 250cc and 350cc classes, alongside Les Graham. His best results of that season came at the Swiss Grand Prix where he finished fifth on the 250 bike, and came home second on the 350 behind his illustrious team mate; he also finished fourth in the 350cc race at Spa. Soon after, Graham signed for the Italian MV factory and Sandford joined him for the 1952 season. Cecil was chosen to ride the ultra lightweight 125cc machines and made a good start to his season with a win at record speed in the two-lap TT race, which he followed with two more victories in Holland and Ulster. Additional third places from the German and Spanish rounds brought Sandford the 125cc World Championship title – the first in that class to be claimed by a British rider, and also the first ever championship win for MV.

Still with Count Agusta's team for 1953, Sandford finished third in the 125cc TT, and also at

the Dutch. He came home second in the Ulster and Spanish races, scoring sufficient points for second place in the world table. After the tragedy of Graham's fatal TT crash, the MV team was demoralised and, although Cecil rode the improved 500 four cylinder, his best result was a disappointing fifth place at Monza, behind the Gilera team. The following season, he was again third in the 125 TT, but managed no better in any of the other classics.

In 1955, Sandford switched to Moto Guzzis and produced some creditable performances on the redesigned works singles. On the Isle of Man, he finished second in the 250 race and third in the Junior, ending the season third in the 250 rankings.

The next year, Cecil switched to yet another factory team, DKW, whose two-stroke 350s he raced with some success, and even found time for rides on a works 125cc FB Mondial. On the DKW, he finished fourth in the 350cc championship.

Teamed up with Sammy Miller on the Mondials for 1957, Sandford won the 250 TT, after Sammy had fallen on the last lap. He also won the Ulster Grand Prix and finished second, third and fourth in other races which took him to his second world title. He had once again become the first British rider to win a class title, this time the 250. After only seven years of international road racing, Cecil Sandford then retired from the sport, while at the peak of his achievement. GE

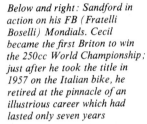

Below and right: Sandford in action on his FB (Fratelli Boselli) Mondials. Cecil became the first Briton to win the 250cc World Championship; just after he took the title in 1957 on the Italian bike, he retired at the pinnacle of an illustrious career which had lasted only seven years

Cyril Smith

Right: Cyril Smith, one of only three Englishmen to have won the World Sidecar Championship. He won the title in 1952

Far right top: Smith and passenger Eric Bliss hurl their Norton Watsonian outfit through a bend at Oulton Park in 1957

Far right bottom: Smith and Bliss again, this time on their fully faired Norton outfit at the Kentish Brands Hatch circuit in 1958

Below: Cyril Smith in action on his 500cc Norton outfit at the Isle of Man Sidecar Tourist Trophy event of 1954

IN MORE THAN thirty years of world championship racing, only three British riders have taken the sidecar title: Eric Oliver, George O'Dell and Cyril Smith. Smith's year was 1952, the year in which he was sacked by Norton . . . for going road racing! Yet, he went on to take the title after Eric Oliver broke his leg in a minor race meeting in France. He was subsequently out of the running for his fourth title in a row.

Cyril Smith was born in Birmingham and started his racing career after coming out of H.M. Forces in 1949 following distinguished war service with the Eighth Army in the Western Desert. He first took to grass track racing, riding passenger for racers like Tommy Woods and Bill Boddice, the first outfit of his own being an Ariel. He ventured into road racing in 1950 and for a time combined both branches

of the sport. His first serious excursion into road racing was in 1951 when he travelled to Belgium, finishing fourth in the grand prix on his home-built Norton Watsonian outfit. The very next year he became world champion, in what was his first full season of serious competition. It was a remarkable performance for a rider with so little experience of international racing, yet the season started disastrously. A crash in practice at Mettet in Belgium left him with a cracked skull and other injuries and he was told he would never ride competitively again. Only three weeks later, he was setting himself up for a full grand prix programme. Driving brilliantly, he was second with passenger Bob Clements in Switzerland, third in Belgium, first in Germany, second in Italy and third in Spain, to take the title.

Although good enough to win a world title, Cyril Smith was always out of luck on the Isle of Man. He raced there every year from 1954 to 1959 and didn't finish once. He came nearest to victory in 1955 when he crashed while in second place.

A determined bid to hold on to his world title for a second year ended in disappointment in 1953 when, despite fine riding and a win in Ulster, he surrendered the crown to Eric Oliver. In 1954, with new passenger Stanley Dibben, he was third in the world championships, and was fifth in 1955; he was fifth again in 1958. He raced until 1959, by which time German BMW machinery was so superior to Smith's Norton that his talents as a sidecar racer were overwhelmed.

Pipe-smoking, round-faced, balding, only 5 feet 5 inches tall and thickly set, Cyril Smith did not look the archetypal world champion, but was an excellent fitter and an extremely good rider. His positive personality was the exterior to a deep thinking, complex individual.

Among many race distinctions were his lap records at the Nürburgring and Silverstone, the former being unbeaten for several years. He had the chance to switch to more competitive Italian machinery, but was unresponsive to approaches from both Moto-Guzzi and Gilera. He was a dedicated patriot and insisted on riding British. Something of an unsung hero, Cyril Smith died in 1962, aged 46.　PC

Percy Tait

PERCY TAIT made his name as one of the most popular and enduring racers on the British scene. Born in 1929, he entered his first road race in 1951 on a Frank Baker Triumph, finishing in second place in the 250cc event at the Hutchinson 100 meeting at Silverstone. Twenty years later, at the age of 42, he was still racing successfully, perhaps reaching the peak of his long career with an astonishing series of rides which brought him the 1971 *Motor Cycle News* Superbike Championship, victory in the Bol D'Or 24 hours marathon (with co-rider Ray Pickrell), the Thruxton 500-mile race (with Dave Croxford), and in the 750cc British Championship. In 1975 he finished second to Chas Mortimer in the 1000cc Open Classic UU on a 750cc Yamaha, a remarkable achievement, at 46 years of age.

During his long career, the evergreen Birmingham rider has concentrated on British machinery. Three years after his first road race, he was sixth in the 500cc Clubman's TT of 1954 and that same year, on the Isle of Man for the Manx Grand Prix, he finished ninth in the Junior event and was running third on a Bob Foster Norton when he had to retire with stripped bevel gears.

Tait was never at his best in the TTs. He first entered in 1955, finishing fifteenth, on an AJS, in the Junior and retiring on the Norton in the Senior, after crashing at speed near Hillberry. He raced ten times in the TTs in the next sixteen years, suffering seven retirements. In 1971 he reached fourth place. Then came his second place in the Open Classic race in 1975. John Williams on the 350cc Yamaha won in a time of 2hrs 8mins 56.8secs, at a race average of 105.33mph. Tait averaged 102.19mph, finishing only 2.4 seconds behind the winner and 26 seconds ahead of third place rider Charlie Sandby.

On the mainland and in other events, Percy Tait did better, his success established as early as 1961 when he won the ultra-lightweight class in the one-event British Championships. Although achieved at an age when most road racers have retired, his surprising successes in the 1970s were particularly significant. When the Anglo-American Match Race Series was established in 1971. Tait wasan automatic choice for the British team. He was there when Britain took the title for the fourth year in succession, in 1974, and also when the United States gained their

first victory the following year. The veteran racer continued to attract attention around the mid 1970s and, in a three-year flurry, he not only raced to second place in the Open Classic TT of 1975 but also, in 1974, won the 1000cc Production event at the John Player International Grand Prix on a Triumph, won the 1000cc class of the Ulster Grand Prix on a Yamaha in 1975, and raced to victory in the 750cc class of the classic North West 200 on a 750cc Suzuki.

After Percy Tait finally retired he kept close to the racing scene. At the end of 1976 he was making plans to form his own team and in 1977 the veteran racer received the singular honour of becoming the first non-riding captain of the British team for the Transatlantic Trophy Series.   PC

Below: Tait in action on the three-cylinder Triumph 750 at Silverstone in 1971. He is now perhaps best remembered for his impressive performances on these machines. 1971 saw Percy win the prestigious Motor Cycle News Superbike Championship

Below right: Percy Tait on his 500cc Norton during a race at Crystal Palace in 1953

Far right centre: Tait (500 Seeley) leads Ray Pickrell at Brands Hatch in 1970

Far right top: Percy on his way to sixth place in the Senior Clubman's TT of 1954 on his 500cc BSA

Far right bottom: Tait displays his style on yet another Triumph machine, a 650cc Triumph Bonneville production racing model. The year is 1966 and the event is the 500 miler held at the Brands Hatch circuit in Kent

Luigi Taveri

Far right top: before riding for Honda, Taveri was contracted to MV. He is seen here on the immaculately faired 125cc Agusta bike

Far right bottom: on the Island again, this time for the 1962 125TT. The machine Luigi is riding is a Honda

Below: Luigi Taveri is seen on the miniscule 50cc Honda at Parliament Square practising for the 1966 TT; he came second in the race

THE DIMINUTIVE racer Luigi Taveri was the greatest Swiss solo rider and was the winner of three world championships and countless grands prix in most countries. In 1954, his first international season, Taveri rode Nortons and a 250cc Ducati with some success, and also passengered fellow Swiss H. Haldemann in the sidecar class. In the Swiss GP, Luigi finished fourth on the Ducati and sixth in the outfit.

His promise as a solo rider was noted by the MV team who signed him up for the 1955 season. On their 125cc machine, he won the first grand prix of the year in Spain, then followed up with three second places to finish the season runner-up in the world championship behind his team-mate Ubbiali. After winning the controversial Dutch round on his 250, Luigi also finished fourth in that class.

The following year, Taveri only won a single grand prix on the 250, and was again second to Ubbiali, while in the 125 class he finished third.

In 1957, he was once more second in the 125 championship, and had also come home second in the 250cc TT. Dropped by MV for 1958, Taveri rode Nortons in the larger classes and a 125cc Ducati, on which he finished third in the final table. He started out the 1959 season with a good second place ride on an MZ in the 125 TT, then scored three more second places on the Ducati and finished the season in fourth spot. His consistency had regained Taveri a place with MV for 1960 but, although he came third in the 125 TT, his best rides were on the 250 bikes on which he ended the year in third place.

When MV quit the lightweight classes, Honda moved in, and Taveri was signed to ride the Japanese machines in 1961. On the 125 bikes, he finished second in the TT and first in Belgium and Sweden, although his points score only brought him to third spot overall. The 1962 season was more successful: after several years of runner-up spots, Luigi won his first TT, and followed up with five other wins on the new 125cc Honda twins to take his first championship. He had also finished third in the first ever 50cc title chase. From then on, Taveri brought 125 world titles to Honda on alternate years, with good places in other classes in between. In 1963, he finished second in the 125 title and third in the 350, but he also scored some fine places on the 250 four-cylinder bikes and a win in the Japanese 50cc race.

In 1964, Luigi took the new four-cylinder 125cc Honda to five first places, including the TT, and four second spots to rake in his second world title. The following season the class was dominated by two-strokes, with Taveri finishing fifth behind the Suzuki and MZ teams. He did win the 50cc TT, however, and the Japanese GP, to add another championship runner-up to his credit.

Honda introduced their five-cylinder 125 machine in 1966, and in the hands of Taveri it proved more than a match for his closest two-stroke rival, Bill Ivy. Taveri took his third title, and another third in the 50cc, and retired from the sport at the peak of his career, to run a motor cycle business in Switzerland. GE

Rolf Tibblin

ASK ANY VETERAN motocross enthusiast what he remembers most about Rolf Tibblin and you will get one of a variety of answers. Probably towards the bottom of the list will come the truly unique fact that Tibblin is the only rider who has held both the 250cc and the 500cc motocross world titles. Admittedly the 250 championship, which he won for Husqvarna in 1959, was designated 'European' but it was a world title in all but name.

Tibblin is far better remembered as the giant of the 500 brigade, where he took the world crown in 1962 by beating his fellow countryman Sten Lundin. The following year Rolf, still faithful to Husqvarna, won the world championship again, in fine style. The French Grand Prix of that year provides a perfect example of his supremacy. The likeable Swede

stormed to victory in both races, held at St. Quentin, to win overall. In doing so he beat Britain's Jeff Smith, the man who was to take his title away from him in 1964, and two previous champions, Bill Nilsson and Sten Lundin.

France was to be a happy hunting ground for Tibblin, no doubt helped by memories of his fantastic win there in 1960, when, as the reigning 250 champion, he was leading the 500 class, having already won the opening round in Austria. The day started hot and dusty but, later, torrential rain turned dust into mud and water-splashes into lakes. Rolf rode the hazards to win the first race and take runner-up spot in the second, giving him overall victory. Although he was denied the title that year – it went to Bill Nilsson – everyone knew it was only a matter of time before that elusive world crown would be rightfully his.

In 1964 he changed his machine. This, however, was not quite such a drastic step as it may at first have appeared to be. Tibblin's Husqvarna had been looked after by his near-neighbour, brilliant engineer Nils Hedlund, and Hedlund had now made his own machine. Rolf declared: 'It's the most beautiful bit of engineering I've ever seen'. He literally put his money – and skill – where his mouth was, when he made a financial investment in the venture and rode the model in the 1964 championship. He came within a hair's breadth of winning too.

Tibblin was to return to Sweden to ride in a relatively insignificant event when the last grand prix of the season was only a week away. He was neck-and-neck on points for the title with Jeff Smith and made the marathon trek from his home in Stockholm to Spain with only 36 hours to spare. Ill prepared, tired and forced into a last minute panic to get better quality petrol, Tibblin lost his chance of retaining the title.

For the next two years he campaigned a CZ. At the 1965 Moto Cross Des Nations he signed the Rickman-Lundin petition to 'save the full-blown 500 class' when, at the time, he was doing nicely on a 360 two-stroke. Eventually, Rolf retired from big-time motocross and went to America to promote Husqvarna machines and there he stayed.   RB

Above: Rolf with 250 Husqvarna at the Coupe D'Europe at Beenham Park in 1959

Far left: Rolf is seen with his Hedlund at Prerov in Czechoslovakia in July 1964

Stanley Woods

Right: Woods being chaired by fans after his spectacular win for the Norton team in the Isle of Man Senior TT of 1926

Far right: apart from his victories for Norton, Woods also rode a variety of machines including Velocette, New Imperial and Scott

MOTOR CYCLE racing between the wars was full of dash and natural vigour. Bikes were simpler, Norton was supreme, and Stanley Woods was everybody's hero. He became a legend in the vintage years of the sport, his jaunty personality and natural skills making him a top celebrity and a consistent motor cycle race winner for more than a decade.

Many are convinced that he was the greatest rider of all time. He was arguably the greatest all-rounder, for he was a winner in virtually every branch of the sport: speedway, long distance record attempts, hillclimbs, scrambles, trials, grass track and even sand racing. It was as a road racer supreme, however, that he built his reputation into a legend. In the nine years from 1930 he won almost forty international events in Britain and abroad. He raced on the Isle of Man for eighteen consecutive years (in itself a record) and won ten TTs, a feat beaten only by Mike Hailwood and equalled by one other, Giacomo Agostini. In the Ulster Grand Prix, then the world's fastest race, he was unbeatable on seven occasions.

Born in Dublin, Woods competed in his first TT as a Cotton works rider in 1922 when he was only seventeen. In the Junior event, his engine caught fire, a push rod flew out and his brakes were less than perfect; yet he finished fifth. He won the event the following year and his phenomenal career was well and truly on its way.

Over the next sixteen years he rode a wide variety of machines including New Imperial, Scott, Blackburne, OK, Royal Enfield, Douglas and Ariel. He signed for Norton in 1926 and won the Senior TT that year. His stay with the famous British factory lasted eight years, 1932 and 1933 being notable for supreme performances on the Isle of Man. In both years he scored Senior and Junior double victories, putting up the fastest lap in the Junior of 1932, and in both the Senior and Junior races of 1933. He left Norton, because he opposed their 'riding to team

orders' policy, and signed for Moto Guzzi. With the Italian factory he scored a Senior/Lightweight TT double in 1935, also setting fastest laps in each race. His unrivalled record at the time was three TT doubles in four years and five out of a possible six fastest laps.

For the last few years of his racing career, Woods switched to Velocette. He won the Junior TT in 1938 and '39 and was second in the Senior and Lightweight events in 1938. That year he narrowly missed another double after an unsuccessful battle with Harold Daniell in the Senior.

The war brought premature retirement, but the legend lived on. Eighteen years after his retirement, Woods took a second string Guzzi round the TT course at 86mph for the Jubilee celebrations of the TT and Stanley was also there to greet Mike Hailwood when he surpassed his record of ten TT victories.   PC

Below: Stanley Woods in action on his 500cc Norton during the Senior TT of 1932. He went on to win the race in impressive fashion

Jack Young

JACK YOUNG was the first and so far only second division rider to win the World Speedway Championship, and he was also the first rider to win this coveted title two years in succession. These two great achievements occurred in the 1950s, when the Australian was acknowledged as one of the greatest of all time.

Maximum points became a speciality of his, and Jack won the Scottish Riders' Championship. After a successful season, he travelled back home for the Australian terms racing.

In his first year, 'Youngie' had topped the Edinburgh score-chart with 278 points, and when he returned, his progress was watched with amazement and admiration. Up and down the country he broke many track records, scored maximum after maximum and ended up with the best record in all three divisions. Jack performed heroic deeds for Australia in that season's England *versus* Australia Test series and now his eyes were fixed on speedway's blue riband, the world title. In the Belle Vue round, he outpaced an international field and gained maximum points, and then at New Cross he just failed to add another £50 bonus cheque to his earnings. However, he had the distinction of being the first rider to be assured of a place in the 1950 World Final at Wembley, such was the remarkable rise to fame of the 25-year-old one-time market gardener from Adelaide.

Topping the score chart once again with 282 points for his side, Jack was also in possession of the Edinburgh track record and the Scottish Riders' Championship. He was the highest scorer in the Britain *versus* Overseas contest, too.

It was not surprising to see Jack as captain of the Edinburgh team in 1951. That season was hardly six weeks old but the incredible 'Youngie' had created speedway history by recording ten successive maximums in North Shield engagements. At Edinburgh's first May meeting, the 15,000 crowd gave the illustrious Australian a terrific ovation when he clocked his ninth maximum. His brilliant rides were made under difficult *conditions*, too, for he had injured his thigh and leg two weeks previously at Wimbledon, injuries which were aggravated by continual riding.

Jack Young and his Mitchell-tuned, JAP-engined machine proved to be a combination which carried all before it, and many thought his magnificent performances were comparable to those of Vic Duggan in 1948. As partner to the renowned Ronnie Moore, he was top scorer for his country in the first Test Match (England *versus* Australia) at Harringay – a match which provided 27,000 spectators with endless thrills and with almost every race having a sprinkling of drama and plenty of action.

Jack's team, the 'Monarchs', won the North Shield again and few teams have emulated their success with only a single defeat in ten matches. His greatest honour so far was the captaining of the Australian team at Wembley, watched by no less than 54,000 spectators.

Jack's winning ways miraculously continued unrelentlessly throughout 1951. He won the Scottish Championship for the third successive year. With clockwork monotony, the diminutive conqueror from Australia cleaned up prize-money and trophies, too, and held the division two Match Race Title for most of the season.

Early in 1952, the Edinburgh skipper was transferred to West Ham for a record transfer fee of £3750, which stood for well over twenty years. He mastered Split Waterman in the Match Race Title and his consistent riding was simply amazing. For the second consecutive year, this star from Adelaide won the World Championship, and the South Australian was acknowledged as one of the speedway greats, and for several years the West Ham team revolved around him. Then in 1956, when West Ham withdrew from the first division, Jack skippered the Coventry side and his superb riding was again clearly evident.

Eventually, in every rider's life, there comes a time of decision, a decision to retire from the sport. It came to Jack Young in the early 1960s and he returned to his native Australia for good, leaving behind him one of the greatest of all speedway records.   CM

Below: Jack Young (far left) at the England versus Australia test at Wimbledon in 1950

Right: Jack Young warms up his machine prior to another test match encounter

THE END

Index

Bold type indicates that an entry is the subject of a feature and shows the pages on which the feature occurs. Italic type indicates an illustration reference. This section also includes a list of the errors made in *The World of Motorcycles.*

Gaastra, Andries: *101*, 101
Gaby: 2185
Gagni, Pietto: *677*
Gaillon hillclimb: 2148
Gall, Karl: 144, 146, 483, 669
Galloway, Billy: *1665*, 1665, 1666, 1667, 1668
Garcia, Bernard: 615
Garelli: 136, **633–637**, 847, 2197, 2200, 2201, 2210; Adalberto, 2733, 2754, 2198, 2203, 2424
Gariglio: 2506
Garrard: 2151
Garsuade, David: 1230
gasket: **639–642**
Gawley, Jeff: 78, 79
Gazelle: 1611
GB: 2160
gears: **643–658**, 1828–1831
gearbox: **647–655**, 1112, *1828*, 1829, 1830, 1831, 2462
gearbox maintenance: **652–655**
gear changing: **656–658**
Geboers, Sylvain: **659–660**, 1431, *1753*, 2047
Geiger: 2160

Geisenhof, Hans: *2114*
Geiss, Arthur: 417, *418*, *2258*
General Electric Company: 1856
generator: **661–666**
Genoud, Alain: *507*
Geoghegan, Maurice: 1596
George, Alex: 173, 186, 346, *385*, 508, 1000
George, Sydney: 2054
German Grand Prix: 30, 52, 121, 125, 140, 172, 173, 459, **667–671**, 733, 766, 797, 879, 880, 1059, 1060, 1097, 1148, 1151, 1208, 1222, 1265, 1328, 1474, 1482, 1483, 1512, 1513, 1514, 1524, 1587, 1740, 1879, 1943, 2042, 2209, 2227, 2247, 2265
German, Howard: 1841
Gherzi, Pietro: 335, 1093, *2210*
Gibson: 2136
Gibson, Hugh: 1372
Gibson, Peter: *938*
Giffard, Pierre: 2117
Gilera: 39, 40, 118, 138, 162, 228, 459, 471, 483, 484, 485, 523, 612, 669, 670, **672–682**, 684, 718, 848, 1040, 1052, 1066, 1088, 1355, 1448, 1585, 1586, 1598, 1645, 1647, 1728, 1738, 1754, 1768, 1819, 1862, 1883, 2042, 2050, 2051, 2056, *2164*, 2232, *2262*, 2266, 2273, 2281, *2295*, 2296, 2298, 2301, 2306, 2312, 2317, 2318, 2336, *2336*, 2337, 2361, 2370, *2370*, 2424, 2465
Giles, F. W.: 2201, 2204, 2209
Giles, Johnny: 1838
Gillard, Richard: 1278, 2203
Gillet: 2159, 2193
Giovanni: 1273
Girard: 2198
Giro d'Italia: 2366
Giro, Eduardo: 1248
Giro, Manuel: 1248
Giulietta: 43
Giuppone, Giosue: 2156, 2157, 2160, 2164
G-L: 2189
Gladiator: 2118, 2119, 2144, 2182
Glanfield, Stanley: 1665
Gleave, Syd: 2236, *2236*
Gloria Cycles: 1848
gloves: 1493, 2470
Gnessa, Ernesto: 634, 2200, 2201, 2203
Gnome and Rhone: 9, 1446, 2187, 2188, 2193
Gobiet, Jules L.: 1455
Goddard, Ian: 451
Goddard, S.: 1836
Godden, Don: 697, *698*, *1997*, 2000

Godfrey, Oliver, C.: *818*, 2167, 2168, 2181
Godfrey, Tony: 1791
Godrey Trophy: 2054
Godier, Georges: *506*, *507*, 892
goggles: 1492, 2169
Gognet: 2146
Golden Helmet Trophy: 876, 1247, 1601, 1602, 1668
Golem: 2188
Gollner, Bob: 1577
Good, Terry: *1576*, 1982
Goodman, Bertie: 484
Goodman, Eugene: 1910, 1911
Goodman, Percy: 1907, *1909*, 1911, 1913
Goodman, Peter: 2279
Gordon Bennett Trophy: 1810, 2115, 2148, 2155, 2156
Gorg, Helmut: 419
Goricke: 2159
Goss, Bryan: 1215, 1968
Goss, Neville: 568
Goudard & Mennesson: 1914, 1915
Gould, George: 697
Gould, John: 697
Gould, Rod: 52, 77, 78, 120, 126, 388, *482*, 486, 574, 575, 614, 709, 850, 871, 1648, *1865*, *2066*, 2391, 2392, **2568–2569**
Govaerts: 2425
Goven, Alexander: 2130
GP de France: 2168, 2193
GP des Nations: 2201, 2203, 2206, 2208
GR: 2208
Grable, L.: *1626*
Graf, Ulrich: 2081, 2084
Graham, B. M.: 2279
Graham, Les: 695, 673, 847, 848, 1049, 1147, *1148*, 1645, 1738, *1767*, 1768, *1814*, 1861, 1862, *1863*, 2042, 2043, 2050, 2052, 2279, 2289, 2293, 2298, 2570–2571
Graham, Les Trophy: 1841
Graham, Stuart: 388, 574, 1748, 1753, **2570–2571**
Granath, Bo: 78, 800
Grand Prix d'Endurance: 458, 1789
Grand Prix des Nations: 1037, 1038, 1278
Grand Prix d'Europe: 1761, 1766, 1768, 2254
Grandseigne, Robert, Collection: 2102
Grant, Mick: 59, 60, 62, *81*, 186, 413, 414, **690–691**, 846, 891, *892*, *893*, 1726, *1727*, 1727, 1763, 1791, 1819, 1919, 1920, 2016, 2398
Grant, R. E. D.: 2198
Grant, Ron: 58, 59, 233, 397, 747
Grand Prix: **683–689**, 2042, 2043, 2049,

2050–2052
Grand Prix Riders Association: 77
Grassetti, Silvio: 77, 120, 388, 848, 1646
Grass track racing: **692–698**
Grau, Benjamin: 463, 873, 1649
Greasley, Dick: 711
Great Horseless Carriage Company 2128
Green: 2160, 2173
Green, Gustavus: 1316
Greenland, George: 1983
Greensmith Trial: 1682
Greenwood, George: 870
Greenwood, John, E.: 1452, 1713, 1714
Greenwood, Owen: 1365, 1586, 1961
Greer, Joseph: 1936
Greeves: 49, 55, 557, 592, **702–707**, 1000, 1378, 1635, 1636, 1967, 2048, 2414
Greeves, Bert: 702, *702*, 703, 704, 706, 707, 2339
Gregory, John: 448
Grenfell, Minnie: 1948, 2035
Gri: 2199
Griet: 2148
Griffiths, John: *2414*
Griffiths, Sid: 1674
Griffon: 2147, *2147*, 2148, 2153, 2156, 2157, *2157*, 2159, 2162, *2162*, 2164, 2167, 2182
Grigg: 2188, *2189*
Grindlay, Dick: 795
Grinton: 2200
Grogg, Robert: 1211, 1578, 1983
Grovewood Awards: **708–711**
Grovewood Securities: 170, 708, 709
GSD (Grant Shaft Drive): 2198
Guazzoni: 2424
Guild of Motoring Writers: 570
Guilford, Mike: 1577, 1578, *1981*, 1981
Guillon, W. H.: 1457
Guili, Rene: 508
Gulf Oil: 1674
Gustafson, Charles: 820
Gustafsson, Leif: 389
Gutgemann (Goodman), Johannes: 1903, 1913, 1904, 1905, 2172, 2173
Guthrie, Jimmy: 117, 669, 683, *686*, 845, 1049, 1208, 1489, 1641, 1761, 1767, 1768, *1811*, 2227, 2229, *2229*, 2248, 2249, 2254, 2255, 2257, 2258, 2259, 2263, *2263*, 2265, **2572–2573**
Guy, Derek: 1529
Guzzi, Carlo: *1092*, 2197, 2238, 2239
Gyron: *714*
Gyroscopic theory: **712–714**

Haab, Christian: 2123, 2124, 2133, 2152
Haas, Egbert: 985
Haas, Werner: 612, 670, 1879, 1863, 1941, 2051, **2574–2575**
Hack: 2188
Hack, George: 1473, 1474, 1475, 2267
Haddow, Don: 233
Hadfield, Walter: 730
Hagens, Hubert: 194, 2205
Hagglund: 2378
Hagon, Alf: 349, *442*, 448, 697, *1678*, 1679, *1728*, *2004*, 2005
Hailwood, Mike: 30, 118, 119, 126, 170 *210*, *231*, 232, 349, 386, 388, 399, 460, 485, 486, 500, 570, 573, 571, 573, 574, 613, 669, *669*, 670, 677, 679, 700, **715–718**, 764, 766, 766, 848, 1052, 1151, 1152, *1205*, 1387, 1489, 1490, *1646*, 1646, 1647, 1762, 1790, *1816*, 1819, *1820*, 1871, 1863, 1865, 1941, 1961, *2050*, 2051 2052 2080, 2319, *2319*, 2321, 2325, *2325*, 2330, *2330*,

2332, 2333, *2333*, 2336, 2339, 2340, *2340*, *2341*, 2342, 2343, *2365*, 2381, 2382, *2383*, 2384, 2385, *2385*, 2386, *2387*
Hailwood, Stan: 695, 715
Haldeman, Hans: 1583
Halford, Major Frank: 1850, 1901, 2191
Hall, Basil: 1006
Hall, Captain J. J.: 1935
Hall, Jim: 1263, 1397
Hallé: 2155
Hallman, Torsten: 50, 799, 800, 1089, 1119, 1429, 2047, 2334, 2337, 2377, 2415, **2576–2577**
Halm: 2419
Hammond, Peter: 703
handlebars: **719–720**
handling: **721–725**
Hand, Mick: 1680
Handley, Wal: 207, 482, *585*, 586, 843, 1401, 1404, *1405*, *1472*, 1733, 1734, 1766,

1836, 2199, 2200, 2201, 2203, 2207, 2208, *2209*, 2229, *2236*, 2241, 2258, 2264, **2578–2579**
Hands, George: 224
Hansen, Bob: 888
Handsford, Gregg: 1919, 1920, *2084*, 2400
Hanlon, brothers: 2103
Hansen, Gerry: 1609
Hansen, Morian: 1971
Hansen, Torleif: *894*
Hardiman, Martin: 858
Hard, Peter & Ron: 710
Hardee, Mabel: *2032*, 2035
Hares, Barry: *1508*
Hargrave, Lawrence: 1446
Harley-Davidson: 58, 59, 178, 193, 350, *350*, *353*, 389, 394–399, 448, 486, 576, 585, **726–737**, 738, 847, 852, 1019, 1020, 1075, 1118, 1258, 1259, 1260, 1303, 1379, 1380, 1436, 1541, 1543, 1675, 1697, *1706*, 1922, 1942, 1943, 2054, 2059, *2060*, 2135,

Sopwith, T. O. M.: 6
Sopwith Motorcycles: *8*, *9*, 2187, 2188, 2198
Sorensen, Sven: *1810*
Sourian: *782*
Southampton & District Motor Cycle Club: 1789, 1791
Southern Railways: 2127
Spacke: 2176
Spa-Francorchamps: 117, 120, 913, 1287, **1641–1644**, 2193, 2205, 2207, 2218, 2295
Spaggiari, Bruno: 462, 814, *816*, 2365
Span, Tommy: 482, *1852*
Spandau: 2187, 2196
Spanish Grand Prix: 52, 53, *762*, 765, 871, 874, 933, *1121*, 1147, 1148, 1165, 1327, 1566, **1645–1649**, 1888
Spanish TT: 2178
spark plugs: **1650–1656**, *1650*, 1653, 1865
Sparta: 1898
Sparton: **1657–1660**
speedometer: 643, 833, 834
speed traps: **1661–1662**
speedway: 75, 76, 84, 85, 134, 135, 154–157, 181, 182, 295, 296, 347, 348, 630, 631, 632, 805, 806, 808, 866, 867, 875, 876, 972, 975, 1010–1013, 1053, 1054, 1134, 1135, 1246, 1247, 1301, 1302, 1366, 1601–1603, 1629, 1630, 1631, **1663–1671**, 1772, 1773, 1781, 1782, 2021–2023, 2045, 2046, 2615
Speedway Control Board: 973
Speedway Riders Association: 155
Speedway World Cup: 84, 85, 182, 295, 347, 631, 866, 876, 973, 1010, 1012, 1053, 1054, 1246, 1247, 1602, 1603, 1631, 1670, 1772, 2045, 2046
Speedway World Team Cup: 76, 296, 348, 632, 867, 1301, 1302, 1602, 1629, 1773, 2021, 2022, 2046
Spiegelhoff, Johnny: 395
Spinka, Milan: 808
Splitdorf: 978, 979
Spondon Engineering Co: 1659, 1660, 1897

Spondon frames: 1592, 1593
Sponsors Association: 1672
sponsorship: **1672–1674**
Sportsmen's Club Cup: 2159
Spree Prize: 2218
Spring, Nigel: 2255
Springsteen, Jay: 1116, 1260, 1436, **1675–1676**
sprinting: 447, **1677–1680**
Sprite: **1681–1683**
Squazzini, Ing Giovanni: 1927
Squire: 1574
SRM: 805
SS Cars Ltd: 1997
Stadelmann, Hans: 1496
Stafford: 2188, 2189
Stafford, Kevin: 1922
Stanislav, Václav: 1975
Standard: 2206
Staniland, Chris: 1405
Stanley, G. E.: 1318, 1320, 1618, 1619
Stanley Show: 792, 818, 1179, 1415, 1733, 1903, 2086, 2112, 2129, 2138, 2169
Star: 2105
Starframe: 1707
Starkle, Ernst: 1768
Starkle, Hans: 1768
Starley, James, K.: 66, 1318, 1451, 1452, 2114
Starley, W.: 2139
starter motor: **1684–1685**
Stastny, Frantisek: 385, 386, 388, 612, 1490, 1762
steam: **1686–1689**
Stebel: 780
Steel, Alan: 2013
steering: 92, 144, 148, 713–714, 719–720, **1690–1694**
Steib: 1572
Steinhausen, Rolf: 80, 120, 389, 1524, 1585, 1588, **1695–1696**, 2398
Steinlein, Herrn: 1939
STEP (Schools Traffic Education Programme): 360
Sterky, Paul: 1982

Stevens, Albert John (Jack): 32, 33, 35, 36, 37, 1326, 2167, 2173, 2174, 2228, 2235
Stevens, Fred: 233
Stevens, George: 358
Stevens, J. H.: 1049, 2208, 2242
Stewart: 2168
Stewart, Gwenda: 1049, 1065
Stewart, Lt. Col: 1049
St John's Circuit (Isle of Man): 2156
St George, Stewart: 1665, 1668
Stock: 2206, 2210
Stockhill, Les: 1985
Stodulka: 2419
Stoll-Laforge, Inge: 1817, 2036
Stonebridge, Brian: 703, 704, 1088, 1636, 1948, 2323, 2419
Storer, Norman: 703
Storey, Ron: 1321
Strand, Andrew: 2176
Stratton, Spencer: 1665
streamlining: **1697–1700**
Street, Neil: 348
stunt riding: 906–910, **1701–1704**
Sturmey Archer: 338, 339, 477, 645, 794, 796, 1003, 1004, 1373, 1453, *1457*, 1457, 1712, 1848, 1850, 2171, 2182
Sturt, Liz: 2035
styling: **1705–1709**
Suberie, Louis: 2117
Subotin, Vladimir: *1781*
Sun: **1710–1712**, 2320, *2320*
Sunbeam: 667, 902, 903, 995, 996, 1005, 1546, 1620, **1713–1720**, 1766, 1835, 1938, 1946, 1995, 2117, 2168, 2173, 2174, 2181, 2184, 2187, 2189, 2192, 2198, 2201, 2204, 2209, 2214, 2232, 2233, 2247, *2275*, 2276, 2279, 2287
Sunbeam MCC: 1398, 1713, 1935, 2320
Sunbeam Novice Trial: 557
Superbike Championship: 171, 414, 690, 691, 1564, 1566, **1724–1725**, 1753
Surridge, Victor: 1469, 1470

Surtees, Jack: 170, 670, 695, 1737
Surtees, John: 118, 148, 170, 472, 485, 612, 613, 679, 848, *1051*, 1149, 1150, 1151, 1598, 1646, **1737–1740**, 1762, *1815*, 1863, *1864*, 1960, 2050, 2051, 2303, 2307, 2314, 2315, *2315*, 2317, *2317*, 2320, 2321, *2321*, 2325, *2325*, 2329, 2330, 2342
suspension: 528, 721–725, 1114, **1741–1745**, 2416
Superb Four: **1721–1723**
Superbie, Louis: 755, 756
supercharging: 473, 522, 1362, **1728–1732**
Suzuka Circuit: 770, 2333
Suzuki: 46, 58, 59, 60, 61, 62, 77, 183, 184, 185, 349, 399, 400, 451, 480, 485, 523, *556*, 570, 574, 576, 613, 711, 747, 748, 765, 766, 814, 815, 832, *837*, 852, 865, 892, *903*, 911, 912, 930, *934*, 1090, 1152, 1173, 1174, 1194, 1275, *1275*, 1276, 1303, *1355*, 1358, 1359, 1371, 1376, 1387, 1431, *1444*, 1448, 1518, *1566*, 1567, 1634, 1648, *1649*, 1707, 1726, 1727, **1746–1760**, 1819, 1822, 1896, 1919, 1968, 2031, 2048, 2051, 2327, 2331, 2333, 2335, 2336, *2336*, 2338, 2340, *2340*, 2341, 2351, 2356, 2382, 2383, 2385, 2386, 2387, 2388, 2391, *2391*, 2392, 2396, 2397, 2398, 2399, *2399*, 2400, 2416, *2419*, *2424*
Svabb, Antonin: 808
Swain, Beryl: 2036
Swallow: 1573, 2280, 2281, 2293
Swan, Bill: 568
Swedish Grand Prix: 53, 125, 457, 459, 570, 797, 892, 1151, 1162, 1752, 1754, **1761–1764**, 1888
Swedish T.T.: 30, 1060, 1287, 1565
Swift: 2139
Swiss Grand Prix: 38, 121, 124, **1765–1768**, 1948, 2031, 2042, 2050, 2205, 2257, 2265, 2284, 2293
SWM: **1769–1771**, 1838, 1840, 2513
Sykes, A. A.: 1852
Syston Park: 426, 427
Szczakiel, Jerzy: 866, 867, **1772–1773**, 2045

Tabateaux: 2157, *2157*
TAC engine: *2164*
Tacchi, P. G.: 2009, 2164
Tacheny, Jules: 586
Taglioni, Dr Fabio: 457, 463, 1895, *2364*, 2365
Tait, Percy: 57, 59, 60, 61, 399, 813, 1726, 1791, **2612–2613**
Takahashi, Kunumitsu: 1646, 1863, *1864*
Talledega: 46, 90, 254, 255, 1543
Talledega 200: 200, 468, 469, 888

Talon Trials bike: 1983
Tamagni: 2149
Tandon: **1774–1777**, 2289
Tankette: 2188
tappets: 228, 229, **1778–1780**, 1892–1894
Tarabanko, Sergei: *807*, 808, **1781–1782**
Targa Florio: 2168, 2197
Tartarini, Leopoldo: 463, 853, 854, *857*, 2364
Tartarini, Egisto: 853
Taruffi, Piero: 672, 2056, 2057, 2262, 2263, 2266, 2273
Taunax: 2306
Taveneau: 2159, 2160
Taveri, Luigi: 30, 118, 386, 484, 485, 486, 571, 574, 764, 765, 766, *851*, 1149, 1150, 1646, 1747, 1748, 1762, 1863, 2330, 2333, *2334*, 2338, 2382, **2614–2615**
Taylor, A. E.: *1471*, *2203*
Taylor, Charles Lafayette: 310
Taylor, Dave: 1704
Taylor, Doris: 2035
Taylor, Eugene: 1903, 1904
Taylor, Geoffrey: 1997
Taylor, Gue: 1903
Taylor, Harry: 759
Taylor, Percy: 1903, 1904
Taylour, Fay: 1668, 2035
Teague, Henry: 1318
Teledraulic forks: 40, 1005, 1743

telescopic forks: 43, 72, 144, 146, 391, 591, 1005, 1707, 1742
Telford, Thomas: 1422, *1423*
Temple-Azani: 194
Temple, Claude: 194, 1049, 1235, 2054, 2055, 2056, 2204, 2206, 2209
Tenni, Omobono: *1767*, 1768, 2263, 2287
Terre Haute: 46
Terrot: **1783–1786**, 2136, 2168, 2178, 2182, 2184, 2200, *2265*, 2461
Terrot, Charles: 1783
Tessier, S. J.: 98, 100
Tessier, T. H.: 97, 98, 99, 2147
Thacker, Ted: 1836, 2266
Thalhammer, Rudi: 386
Thé: 2147
Thiem: 2134
Thomann: 2189
Thomas, Ernie: 418, 2266
Thomas, Ian: 182
Thomas, R. D.: 1901
Thomas, Réné: 2157
Thompson, Eric: 695
Thompson, S. J. K.: 1833, 1834
Thomson, R. W.: 2115
Thor: 2134, 2176, 2179
Thornhill, Gladys: 1668
Thornton, Joe: *999*
Thousand Mile Trial: 869
Three Musketeers Trial: 1838

throttle: 315, 819, **1787–1788**
Thruxton: 456, 506, 507, 508, **1789–1791**
Thruxton 500: 77, 148, 336, 345, 346, 413, *452*, *504*, *505*, 506, 507, 1791, 2018
Thurow, Gerhard: 120
Tibblin, Rolf: 799, 1086, 1089, 1639, 2047, 2415, *2417*, 2427, 2434, 2437, 2439, *2439*, 2477, **2616–2617**
Tiffen, Bill: 1838, 2256
Tiller, Stuart: *1657*
timing: **1792–1794**, 1863, 1864, 2457
Timmer, Jaap: 1052
Tingey, Richard: 2141
Toersen, Aalt: 613, 912, *914*, 1648, *2084*
Tolksdorf: 2148
Toman: 2156, 2157
Tomasik, Dave: *371*
Tonti, Lino: 23, 139, 140, 1092, 2361
tools: **1795–1798**
Tormo, Riccardo: 2400
torpedo sidecar: *35*
Torres, Ramon: 213
torque: **1799–1800**
Torque Manufacturing Co: 822
Tostevin, Ken: 385
'Tough on a Two-Stroke' (film): 1926
Tour de France Motocycliste: 2158
touring: **1801–1806**
Tour of Italy: 2182
Tourist Trophy (TT): 23, 30, 35, 36, 81, 83,

U V

Errata

Every effort has been made during the compilation of *The World of Motorcycles* to ensure that all the statements made are correct. Inevitably, and due largely to circumstances beyond our control, some errors have crept in. Below is a list of all the errors of which we are aware, and the corrections which should be made.

Page:

9 The maker of the ABC Skootamota was Gilbert Campling and not Gilbert Campion as stated.

33 Early Stevens machines used drive chain only and not belt drive as stated.

40 The reference to a 1954 AJS Porcupine is incorrect. The model was known as the E93 and was substantially different to the original Porcupine machines.

46 The title given to the Dave Aldana article is incorrect. The nickname 'Burrito' belongs to Gene Romero not Aldana.

76 The picture of Martin Ashby was taken at Reading and not Leeds.

91 Photographs of Steve Baker were taken at Mallory Park and not Silverstone as stated in caption.

135 The picture of Terry Betts was taken at Wimbledon and not at Kings Lynn.

154 The picture of Eric Boocock was taken at Wimbledon and not at Coventry.

159 Picture captioned in Brakes article is of a drum brake arrangement on a Puch, not a disc brake as stated.

270 Engine fitted to the AA Chater-Lea pictured was manufactured by Chater-Lea and not Blackburne.

290 In the clutch diagram the words 'the parts in solid black' should be replaced by 'the parts in solid green'.

Page:

296 The action picture purporting to depict Peter Collins at Reading is in fact a photograph of Barry Briggs at Wimbledon.

325 The power figure for the Cossack K58 should read 5.6bhp and not 56bhp as stated in the text.

347 The photograph has been incorrectly captioned. It was taken at the 1976 World Cup Qualifying round at Ipswich and not the 1977 World Final as stated.

361 The caption directions should read Below and Overleaf, not Below and Left.

435 The initials of Mr Barter were J.J. not W.J. as stated in the text.

440 The machine on which Don Chapman won the Junior Clubman's event at Silverstone was a standard Douglas Mark III model and not a 90 Plus.

450 The picture of the customised Dresda is of a 400cc Honda engined model and not a 750.

482 Picture captioned as Rod Gould is incorrect. The rider shown is Derek Minter.

513 The engine illustrated is a Suzuki 750 four, not a Kawasaki 900 as stated in the caption.

518 The examples used to illustrate the diagram of a 60 degree vee-twin engine are all incorrect. Harley-Davidson machines use 45 degree engines, Vincent used a 50 degree configuration while Moto Guzzi engines are of 90 degrees.

534 The rider depicted is Syd Gleave and not S.G. Leare as stated in caption.

535 The Excelsior Manxman model pictured is a single-cylinder machine and not a twin as stated.

600 The Norton Featherbed frame pictured was not replaced in 1956 as mentioned in the caption but continued until the Manx range was discontinued in 1961.

605 The photograph on this page was taken at the Isle of Man and not at Brooklands.

643 Photograph depicts a Z400 Kawasaki twin and not a Z900 four as stated.

644 The picture of worm drive gears shows the tachometer drive on a Z900 Kawasaki and not the speedmeter drive as suggested in the caption.

647 The caption should read 'The drive is merely by an outside belt straight from the belt pulley' and not from the flywheel as stated.

685 Giacomo Agostini is riding a 500cc Yamaha and not a RG500 Suzuki as stated in the picture caption.

697 The picture shows H. Bund and F. Novotny on a 750 Mammoth at Lydden in 1971 and not Jurgen Niebuhr as stated in the caption.

744 The name of the owner of the KJ Henderson pictured has been incorrectly printed. It should read Noel Mavrogordato.

785 Howard R. Davis was sixteen years of age when he made his competition debut and not eighteen.

822 The final paragraph of the Indian article is misleading. The present day Indian models are assembled in Taiwan using engines manufactured in Italy and not as stated.

857 The designer mentioned in the caption is Leo Tartarini, not Tartartini as stated.

975 The picture of speedway rider Dag Lovass was taken at Oxford Stadium and not at Belle Vue as captioned.

997 The photograph on this page was taken at Mallory Park and not on the Isle of Man as stated.

1008 The picture of the G80 Matchless is incorrectly captioned as an overhead camshaft model. It is, in fact, a pushrod machine.

1175 The picture captioned as a 1952 New Hudson auto-cycle is actually of 1941 vintage.

1270 The captions for the top and bottom pictures on this page have been transposed.

1304 The police Triumph pictured is of 1949 vintage and not 1959 as stated.

1305 The machine pictured is a Norton Atlas 750 model of 1964, not a 650SS of 1967.

1308 The Ducati pictured is a parallel twin model and not

a vee-twin as captioned.

1324 The caption for the Ducati Apollo pictured is misleading. It was the Ducati vee-twins that were developed from the Apollo not the Moto Guzzi vee-twins.

1373 The 598cc model mentioned in the text was a single-cylinder machine and not a vee-twin as stated. Also, the 399cc single was developed from a 798cc twin and not 998cc as printed.

1405 The Rex-Acme factory in Osborne Road was closed in 1925 and not 1930 as mentioned on page 1405.

1456 The machine pictured at the top of the page is a vee-twin and not a single as stated in the caption.

1536 The Scott Socialite pictured was developed after World War I and not during it as stated in the caption.

1537 The picture on this page was taken at Ballig Bridge and not Ballaugh Bridge as stated.

1581 The main picture on this page is incorrectly captioned. The rider is George Grinton and the machine is a Norton not a Morgan.

1666 The Douglas speedway machine pictured is a flat twin and not a single as captioned.

1668 The picture caption is incorrect. Eve Askquith is pictured right and not left as stated.

1735 On this page it states that Alec Bennet designed a special head for an OK-Supreme's 250cc JAP engine. The design, in fact, was the work of George Jones.

1855 The Triumph Thunderbird depicted is of 1968 vintage and not 1954 as stated in the caption. The Speed Twin model is also shown on this page and described as a 1956 model is of 1961 vintage.

1858 The fuel tank capacity for the Triumph Bonneville specification should read $3\frac{1}{2}$ gallons (16.0 litres) and not as stated.

1860 The fuel tank capacity for the Triumph Tiger specification should read 4 gallons (18.2 litres).

1903 The capacity of the machine depicted is 220cc and not 211cc as stated in the caption.

1909 The rider depicted is not Percy Goodman as stated in the caption but Peter Goodman.

1911 The photograph on this page was taken during the Senior Manx Grand Prix of 1955 and not during the Senior TT.

2075 In the text reference is made to an SX750 Yamaha. This should have been printed as XS750.

2578 In the Walter Handley feature the following corrections should be made. Handley was 20 years old in 1922, not 18; he joined Rex-Acme in 1923 not 1925 and eventually became a director not competitions manager as stated; his civic reception was at Coventry, not Birmingham.

This magnificent four-color encyclopedia is brought to you by Columbia House in cooperation with Orbis Publishing Ltd., one of Great Britain's most enterprising publishers. Rather than change any of the encyclopedia's authoritative international automotive text, we have included a glossary of terms that will give you immediate American equivalents, and conversion tables for the international metric system.

Glossary

BRITISH	AMERICAN	BRITISH	AMERICAN
Aerial	Antenna	Double knocker	Double overhead camshaft
Aero engine	Aircraft engine		
Aerofoil	Airfoil	Downdraught	Downdraft
Aluminium	Aluminum	Dustbin	Garbage can
Anti-froth baffle	Tank baffle	Dust excluder	Seal
Anti-knock rating	Octane rating	Dynamo	Generator
Apron	Skirt	Earth	Electrical ground
Back-to-front	Backwards	Earthing strip	Ground wire
Back to square one	Start over from the beginning	East-west mounting	Transverse mounting
		End-float	Runout
Badge engineering	Identical bikes with different nameplates (such as the BSA and Triumph brands)	Epicyclic gearbox	Planitary transmission
		Estate car	Station wagon
		Extreme-pressure lubricant	Heavy duty (gear) oil
Bang on	Exactly	Farrier	Blacksmith, horse shoer
Benzol	Benzene	First-motion shaft	Input shaft
Big-end	Larger (crankshaft) end of a connecting rod	Fit	Install
		Flat-out	Top speed
Bi-metal	Bi-metallic	Fore-and-aft mounting	Longitudinal mounting
Blow-back	Backfire in the intake manifold or carburetor	40 years on	40 years in the future
Blower	Supercharger	Gaiter	Rubber boot
Bottle-screw jack	Type of hydraulic jack	Gearbox	Transmission
Box spanner	Socket	Gearchange	Shift pedal or lever (n.) or shift (v.)
Brake horsepower (bhp)	Net horsepower (hp)		
Brake servo	Power brake	Glassfibre	Fiberglass
Bush	Bushing	Glass-reinforced plastic	Fiberglass
		Gudgeon pin	Piston or wrist pin
Capacity	Displacement	Half-liners	Split shell bearings
Carburettor	Carburetor	Half shaft	Axle shaft
Carcass	Tire body or plies	High tension	High voltage
Castellated nut	Castle nut	High-tension leads	Spark plug cables
Chain wheel	Sprocket	Hose clip	Hose clamp
Choke flap	Choke plate		
Clutch release bearing	Clutch throwout bearing	Ignition harness	Ignition cable set
Cogged belt	Rubber timing belt	Immediately	As soon as
Collets	Split collar retainers	Indicators	Turn signals
Conrod	Connecting rod	Induction	Intake
Control box	Voltage regulator	Inlet	Intake
Core plug	Freeze-out or Welsh plug	Jubilee clip	Brand of worm-drive hose clamp
Crash box	Non-synchromesh transmission		
		Judder	Shudder
Crocodile clip	Alligator clip	Jump leads	Jumper cables or wire
Crown wheel	Ring gear	Just on	Exactly
Damper	Shock absorber	Kerb	Curb
Decarbonise	Remove carbon deposits from combustion chamber	Knife cuts	Tire sipes
		Layshaft	Countershaft
De-clutch	Disengage clutch	Leads	Cables or wires
Decoke	See "Decarbonise"	Low-tension	Low voltage
De-ionised water	Distilled water		
Detonation	Pre-ignition	Main beam	High headlight beam, "brights"
Dipped headlight	Low beam		
Dipswitch	High/low beam switch	Marque	Brand, make
Directly	Right away	Midlands	English industrial center
DOE test	A state inspection	Mileage recorder	Odometer

Glossary

BRITISH	AMERICAN
Mileometer	Odometer
Mixture	Fuel-air mixture
Monobloc	Engine with crankcase and cylinder block cast in one piece
Monocoque	Frame constructed of sheetmetal box sections rather than tubes
Motor	Engine
Nave plate	Wheel cover, hubcap
Nil	Zero, nothing
Non-return valve	One-way valve
Number plate	License plate
One-lunger	Single-cylinder
One-off	One-of-a-kind
ONO	"Or near offer" (used in classified ads)
Opposite number	Equal, equivalent, mate
Overrun	Coasting in gear
Paraffin	Kerosene
Perspex	Plexiglas
Petroil	Gas and oil mixture
Petrol	Gasoline
Petrol pump	Fuel pump
Pillion	Passenger saddle or seat
Pinking	Pinging
Plunger	Detent ball
Pocketing	Excess valve seat wear
Pots	Cylinders
Production	Stock
Prop stand	Kick stand
Propeller shaft	Driveshaft
Purpose-built	Special
Quietening ramps	Low acceleration cam profile for quiet engine operation
RAC	Royal Automobile Club
Rear lamp	Tail light
Retrograde step	Step backwards
Rev counter	Tachometer
Ring spanner	Box wrench
Road roar	Tire noise
Rocker	Rocker arm
Rocker box	Rocker or valve cover
Rocker clearance	Valve clearance
Round	Around
Rubber solution	Rubber cement
Running-in	Break in
Running-on	Dieseling
Saloon	Sedan
Scheme	Plan, program
Screen	Windshield
Scuttle	Cowl

BRITISH	AMERICAN
Second-motion shaft	Countershaft
Sediment chamber	Trap
Self-locking nut	Locknut
Servo assisted	Power assisted
Shunt	Accident, bump, crash
Side-draught	Side draft
Side-valve engine	Flathead engine
Slow-running	Idle
Small-end	Smaller (piston) end of a connecting rod
Snap-in valve	Tubeless tire valve
Spade connector	Bayonet connector
Spanner	Wrench
Spigot	Pin
Spit-back	See "blow-back"
Split cones	Split collar retainers
Spot-on	Exactly
Squib	Auto seatback
5 star petrol	100 octane gasoline
4 star petrol	99-97 octane gasoline
3 star petrol	96-94 octane gasoline
2 star petrol	93-90 octane gasoline
Starting handle	Crank
Strangler flap	Choke plate
Sump	Oil pan
Swivel pin	Kingpin
Tab washer	Lock washer
Third-motion shaft	Output shaft
Throttle-stop screw	Idle speed screw
Throttle valve	Butterfly valve
Tick-over	Idle speed
Tin	Can
Tommy bar	Breaker bar, socket wrench
Top end	Cylinder head, or top speed
Trafficators	Early brand of turn signals
Twin-choke carburettor	Two-barrel carburetor
Tyre	Tire
Undo	Remove
Unsymmetrical	Asymmetrical
Venturi	Carburetor barrel
Volume-control screw	Idle mixture screw
Wheel brace	Lug wrench
Windscreen	Windshield
Wing	Fender
Wire wool	Steel wool
Works	Factory
Zinc-oxide grease	Bearing grease

Metric Equivalents
(Based on National Bureau of Standards)

Length

Centimeter (Cm.)	= 0.3937 in.	In.	= 2.5400 cm.
Meter (M.)	= 3.2808 ft.	Ft.	= 0.3048 m.
Meter	= 1.0936 yd.	Yd.	= 0.9144 m.
Kilometer (Km.)	= 0.6214 mile	Mile	= 1.6093 km.

Area

Sq. cm.	= 0.1550 sq. in.	Sq. in.	= 6.4516 sq. cm.
Sq. m.	= 10. 7639 sq. ft.	Sq. ft.	= 0.0929 sq. m.
Sq. m.	= 1.1960 sq. yd.	Sq. yd.	= 0.8361 sq. m.
Hectare	= 2.4710 acres	Acre	= 0.4047 hectare
Sq. km.	= 0.3861 sq. mile	Sq. mile	= 2.5900 sq. km.

Volume

Cu. cm.	= 0.0610 cu. in.	Cu. in.	= 16.3872 cu. cm.
Cu. m.	= 35.3145 cu. ft.	Cu. ft.	= 0.0283 cu. m.
Cu. m.	= 1.3079 cu. yd.	Cu. yd.	= 0.7646 cu. m.

Capacity

Liter	= 61.0250 cu. in	Cu. in.	= 0.0164 liter
Liter	= 0.0353 cu. ft.	Cu. ft.	= 28.3162 liters
Liter	= 0.2642 gal. (U.S.)	Gal.	= 3.7853 liters
Liter	= 0.0284 bu. (U.S.)	Bu.	= 35.2383 liters

$$\text{Liter} = \begin{cases} 1000.027 \text{ cu. cm.} \\ 1.0567 \text{ qt. (liquid) or } 0.9081 \text{ qt. (dry)} \\ 2.2046 \text{ lb. of pure water at 4 C} = 1 \text{ kg.} \end{cases}$$

Weight

Gram. (Gm.)	= 15.4324 grains	Grain	= 0.0648 gm.
Gram	= 0.0353 oz.	Oz.	= 28.3495 gm.
Kilogram (Kg.)	= 2.2046 lb.	Lb.	= 0.4536 kg.
Kg.	= 0.0011 ton (sht.)	Ton (sht.)	= 907.1848 kg.
Ton (met.)	= 1.1023 ton (sht.)	Ton (sht.)	= 0.9072 ton (met.)
Ton (met.)	= 0.9842 ton (lg.)	Ton (lg.)	= 1.0160 ton (met.)

Pressure

1 kg. per sq. cm.	= 14.223 lb. per sq. in.
1 lb. per sq. in.	= 0.0703 kg. per sq. cm.
1 kg. per sq. m.	= 0.2048 lb. per sq. ft.
1 lb. per sq. ft.	= 4.8824 kg. per sq. m.
1 kg. per sq. cm.	= 0.9678 normal atmosphere

$$1 \text{ normal atmosphere} = \begin{cases} 1.0332 \text{ kg. per sq. cm.} \\ 1.0133 \text{ bars} \\ 14.696 \text{ lb. per sq. in.} \end{cases}$$

How to Convert Metric Measurements to U.S. Equivalents

TO CONVERT:	TO:	MULTIPLY BY EXACTLY:	MULTIPLY BY APPROXIMATELY:
Millimeters (mm)	Inches (in.)	0.039	4/100
Centimeters (cm)	Inches (in.)	0.394	4/10
Meters (m)	Feet (ft.)	3.28	3¼
Meters (m)	Yards (yd.)	1.09	1-1/10
Kilometers (km)	Miles (mi.)	0.621	⅝
Kilometers per hour (kph)	Miles per hour (mph)	0.621	⅝
Kilometers per liter (kpl)	Miles per gallon (mpg)	2.352	2⅜
Square centimeters (cm²)	Square inches (sq. in.)	0.155	3/20
Square meters (m²)	Square feet (sq. ft.)	10.8	11
Square meters (m²)	Square yards (sq. yds.)	1.2	1¼
Cubic centimeters (cc)	Cubic inches (c. i.)	0.061	1/16
Liters (1000cc)	Cubic inches (c. i.)	61.025	61
Cubic meters (m³)	Cubic feet (cu. ft.)	35.3	35⅓
Cubic meters (m³)	Cubic yards (cu. yds.)	1.31	1⅓
Liters (l)	Pints (pt.)	2.11	2-1/10
Liters (l)	Quarts (qt.)	1.06	10/9
Liters (l)	U.S. gallons (gal.)	0.264	¼
Liters (l)	Imperial gallons	0.22	2/9
Imperial gallons	U.S. gallons	1.2	1¼
Miles per Imperial gallon	Miles per U.S. gallon	1.2	1¼
Grams (gm)	Ounces (oz.)	0.035	3/100
Kilograms (kg)	Pounds (lb.)	2.2	2¼
Metric tons	Tons	1.1	11/10
Hundredweight (cwt.)	Pounds (lb.)	112.0	—
Stone	Pounds (lb.)	14.0	—
Kilogram-meters (kg-m)	Foot-pounds (ft.-lb.)	7.232	7¼
Kilograms per square centimeter	Pounds per square inch (psi)	14.22	14¼
Metric horsepower (bhp DIN)	U.S. horsepower	0.9859	—

How to Convert U.S. Measurements to Metric Equivalents

TO CONVERT:	TO:	MULTIPLY BY EXACTLY:	MULTIPLY BY APPROXIMATE
Inches (in.)	Millimeters (mm)	25.4	25½
Inches (in.)	Centimeters (cm)	2.54	2½
Feet (ft.)	Meters (m)	0.305	3/10
Yards (yd.)	Meters (m)	0.914	9/10
Miles (mi.)	Kilometers (km)	1.609	8/5
Miles per hour (mph)	Kilometers per hour (kph)	1.609	8/5
Miles per gallon (mpg)	Kilometers per liter (kpl)	0.425	2/5
Square inches (sq. in.)	Square centimeters (cm²)	6.45	6½
Square feet (sq. ft.)	Square meters (m²)	0.093	1/10
Square yards (sq. yd.)	Square meters (m²)	0.836	4/5
Cubic inches (c. i.)	Cubic centimeters (cc)	16.4	16½
Cubic inches (c. i.)	Liters (1000cc)	0.164	4/25
Cubic feet (cu. ft.)	Cubic meters (m³)	0.0283	3/100
Cubic yards (cu. yd.)	Cubic meters (m³)	0.765	¾
Pints (pt.)	Liters (l)	0.473	½
Quarts (qt.)	Liters (l)	0.946	9/10
U.S. gallons (gal.)	Liters (l)	3.78	3¾
Imperial gallons (gal.)	Liters (l)	4.55	4½
Ounces (oz.)	Grams (gm)	28.4	28½
Pounds (lb.)	Grams (gm)	454.0	450
Pounds (lb.)	Kilograms (kg)	0.454	½
Foot-pounds (ft.-lb.)	Kilogram-meters (kg-m)	0.1383	3/20
Pounds per square inch (psi)	Kilograms per square cm	0.0703	7/100
U.S. horsepower	Metric horsepower (bhp DIN)	1.014	—